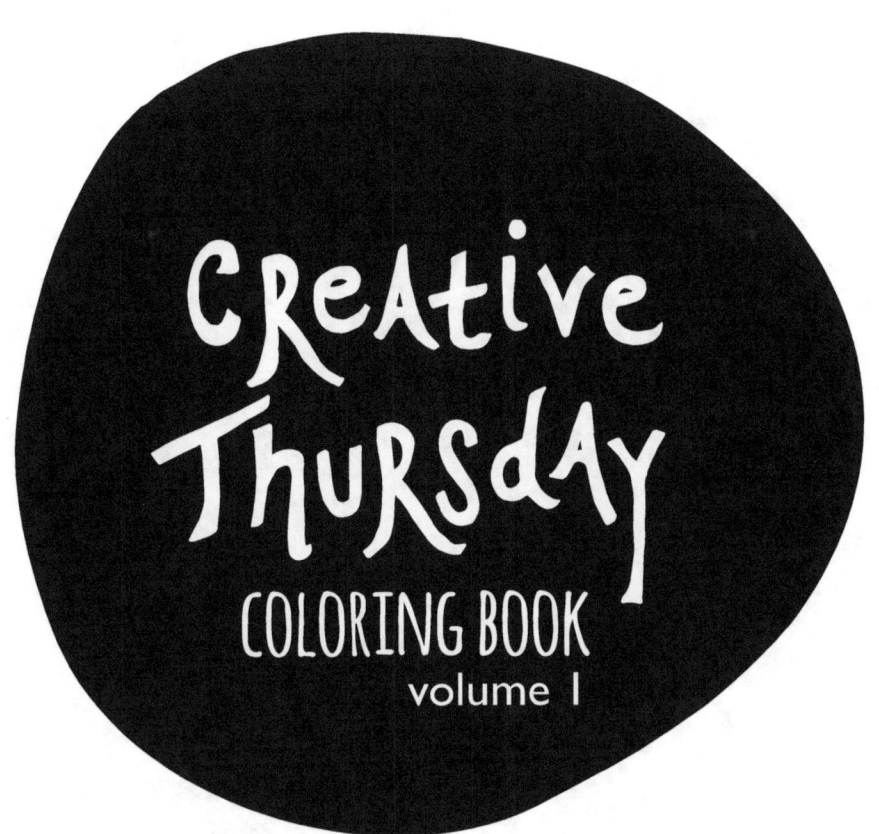

Creative Thursday
COLORING BOOK
volume 1

featuring art by MARISA ANNE CUMMINGS

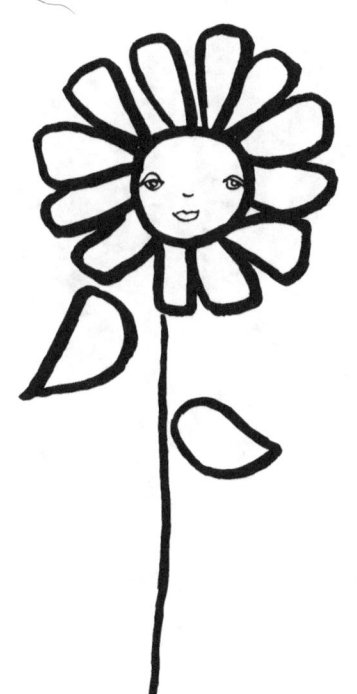

Creative Thursday Coloring Book, Volume 1
© 2004 - 2014 Creative Thursday & Marisa Anne Cummings

www.creativethursday.com

Creative Thursday Press
Los Angeles, CA 90018

Hello! and welcome to the world of Creative Thursday. Just inside
are a whole bunch of friends who can't wait to meet you. There are pictures
and patterns to color, along with plenty of space to add your own drawings
and characters. Use your favorite colored pencils and markers or a variety
of other media. To help prevent bleed-through, place a blank sheet of paper
between the pages when coloring.

happy creating & coloring!

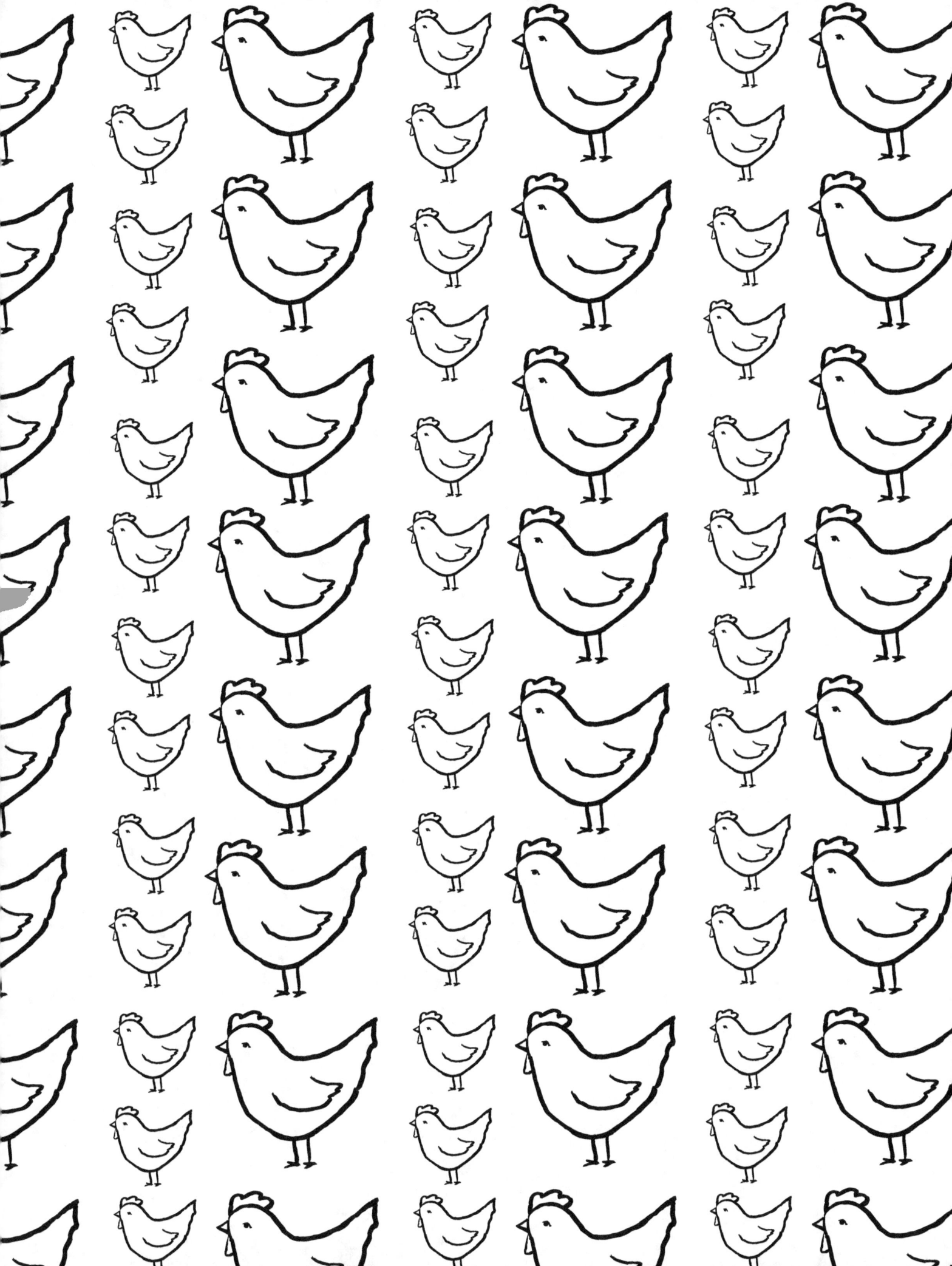

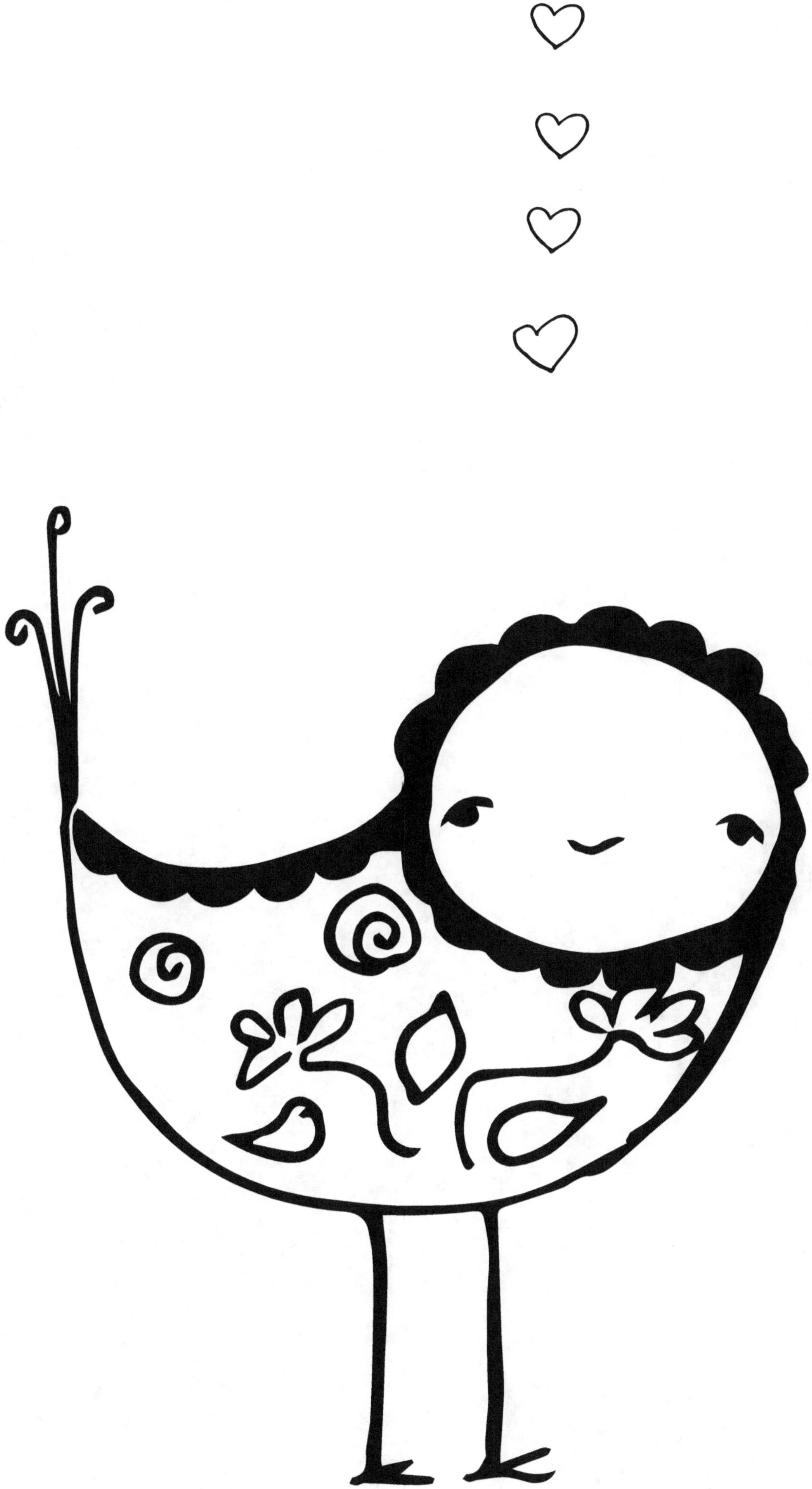

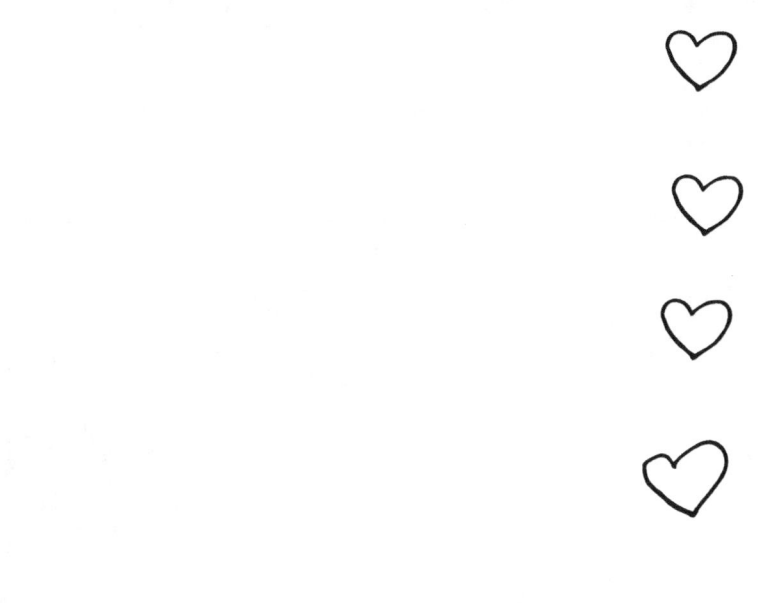

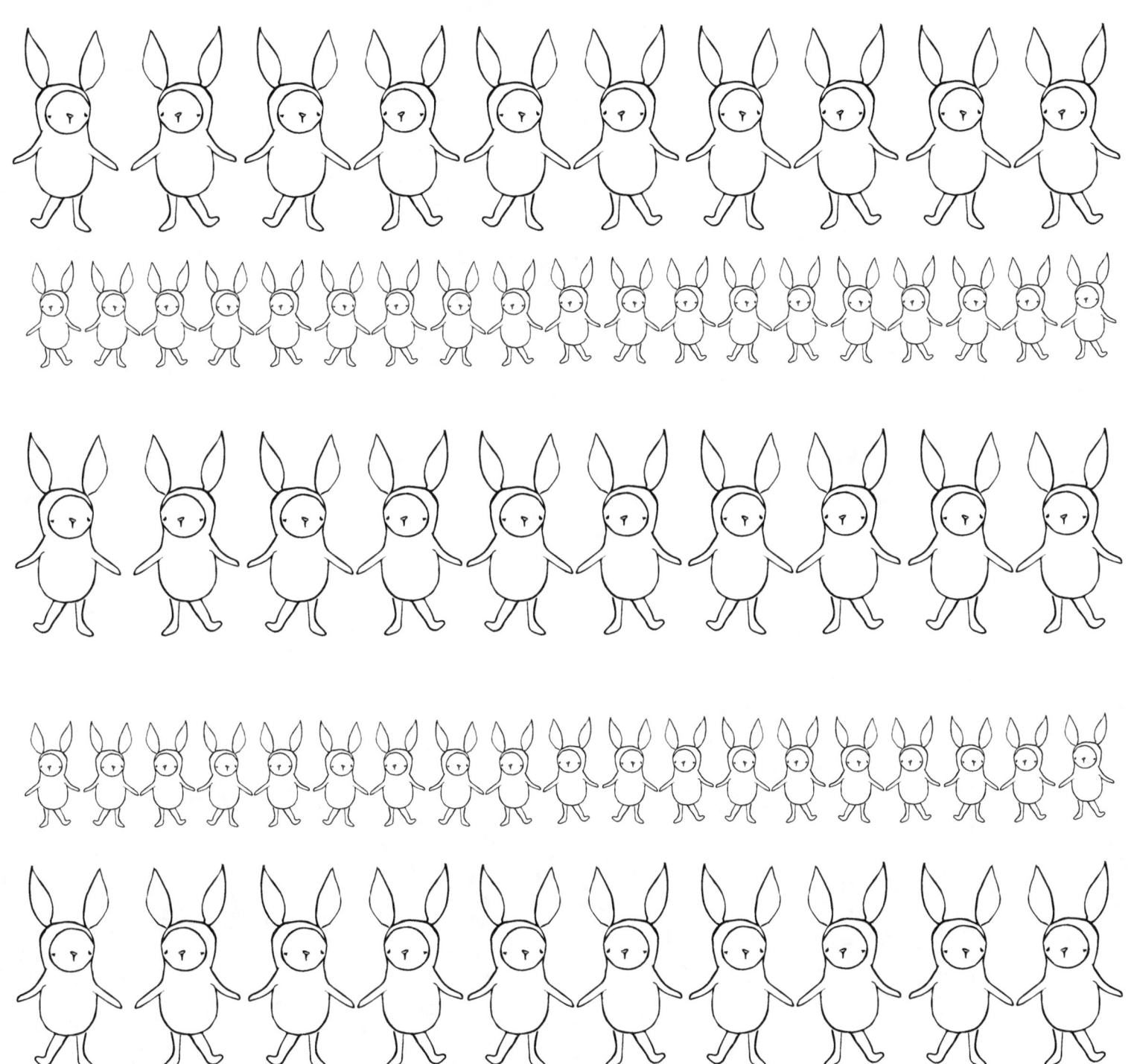

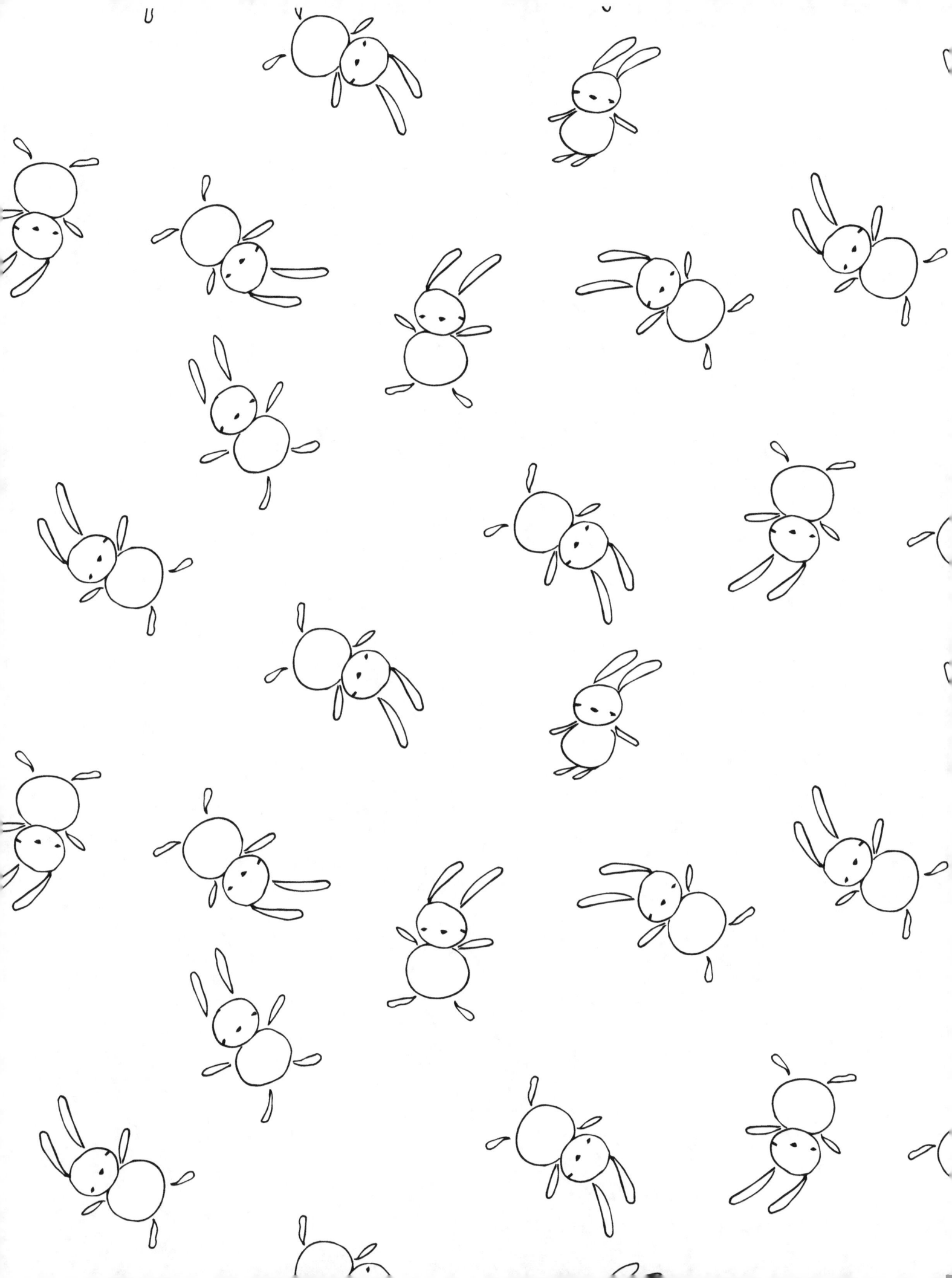

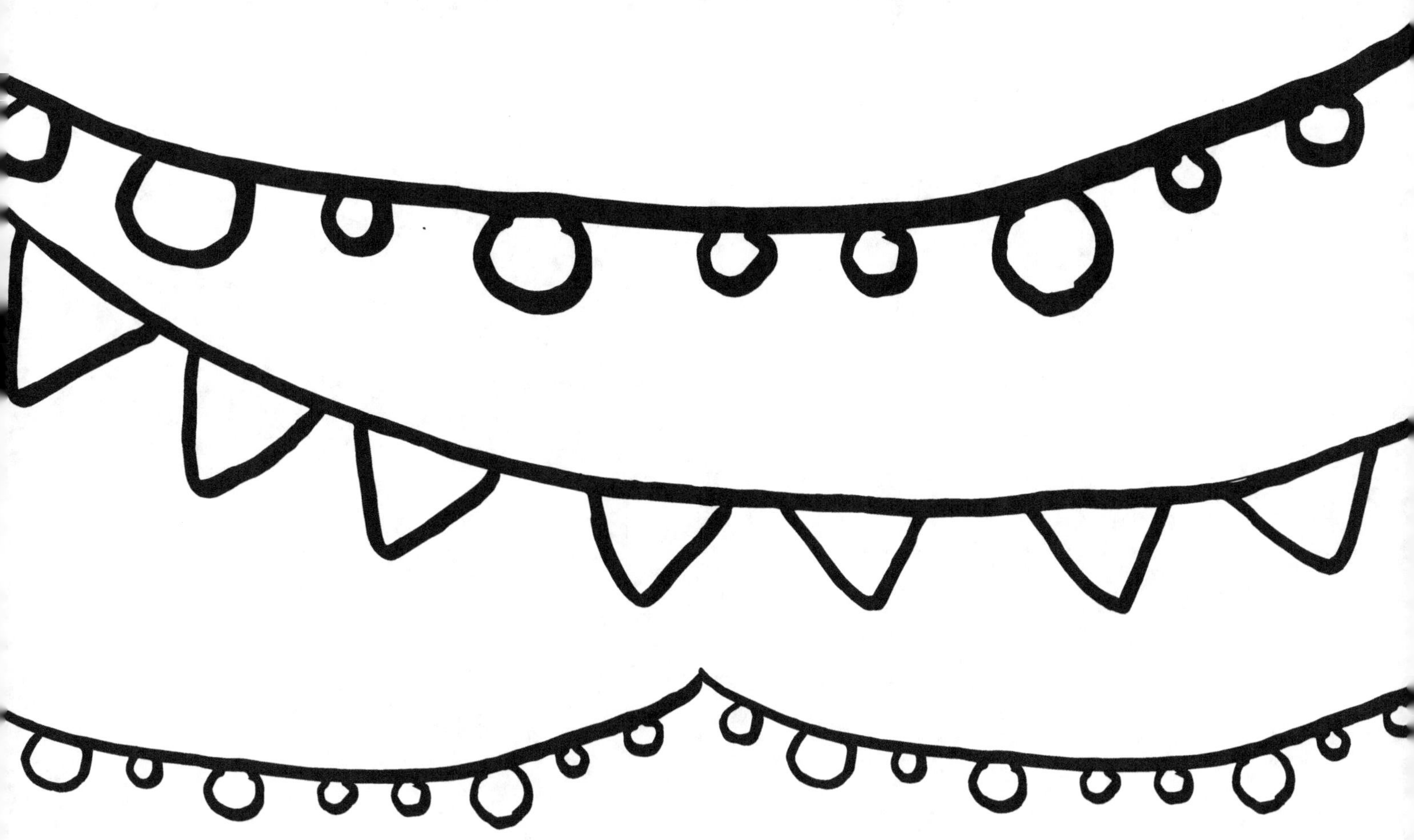

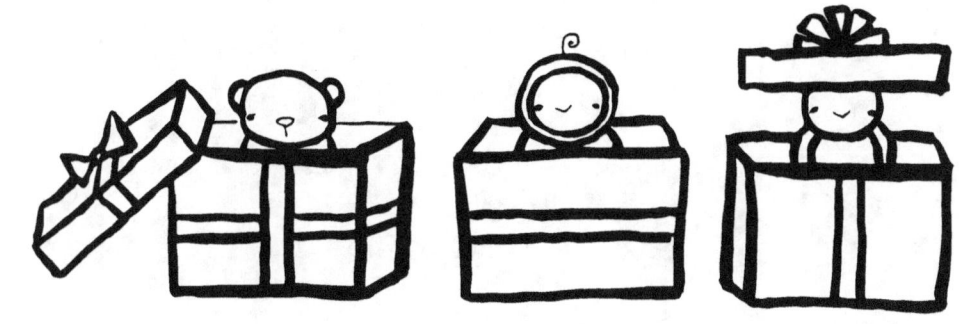

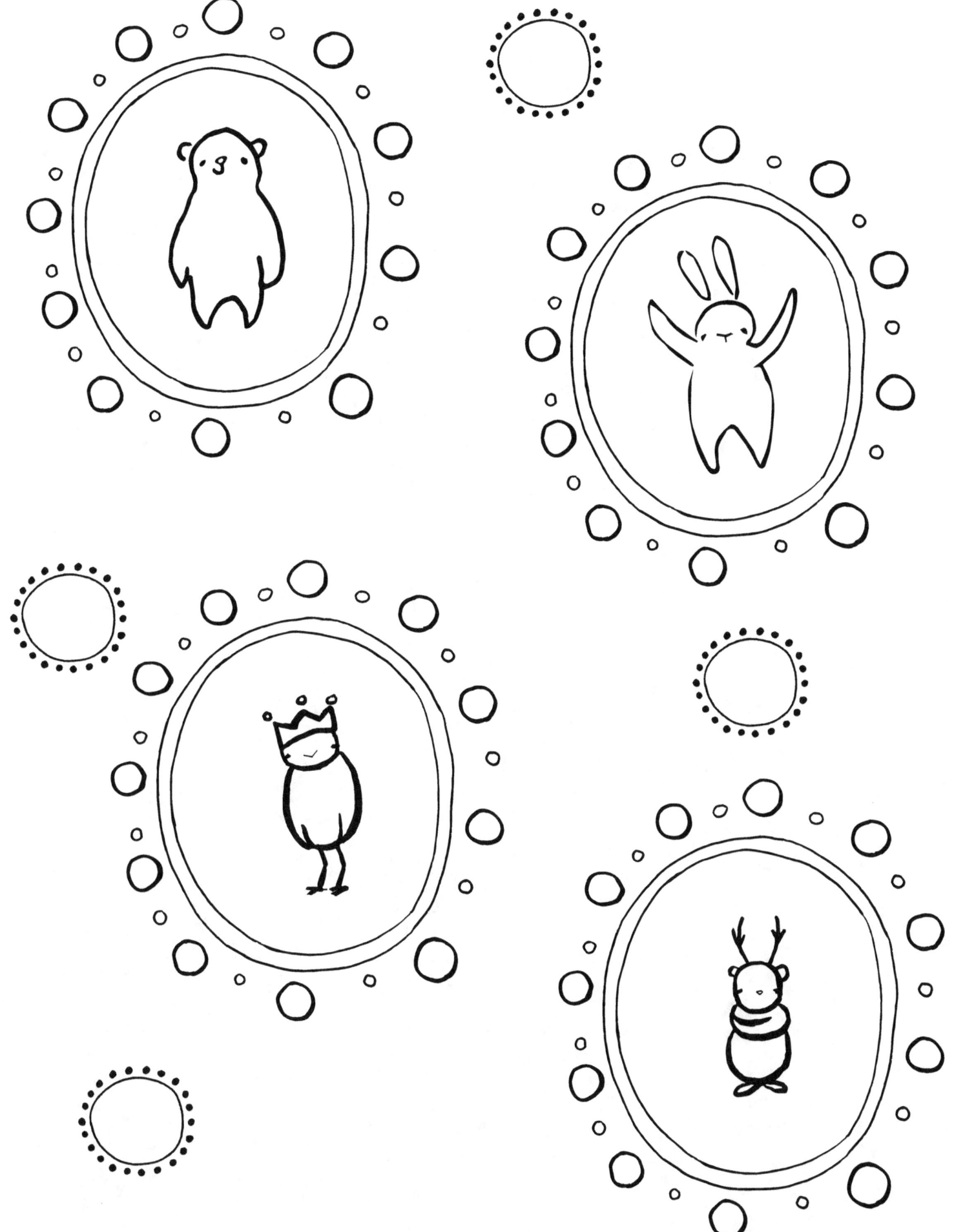

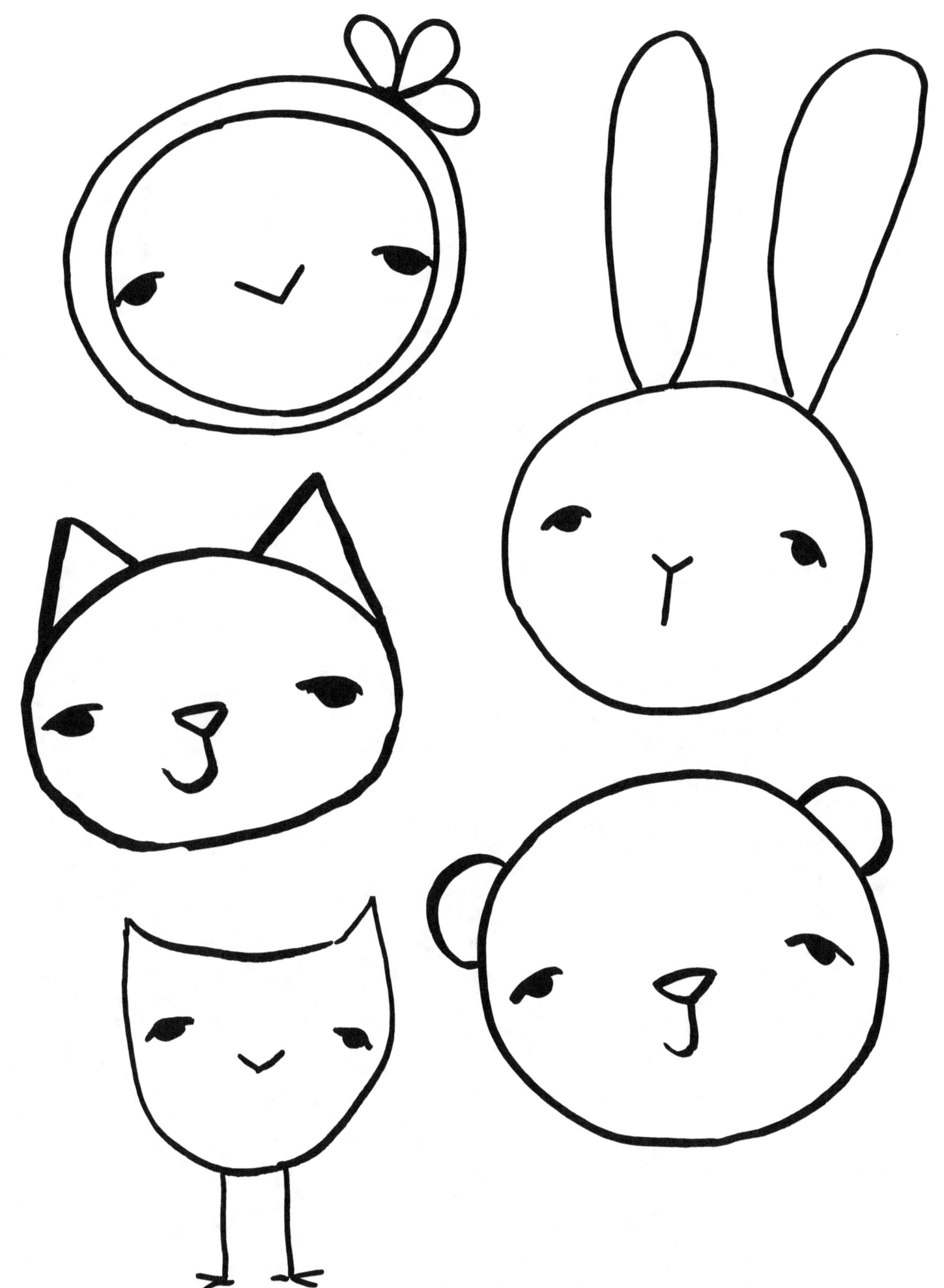

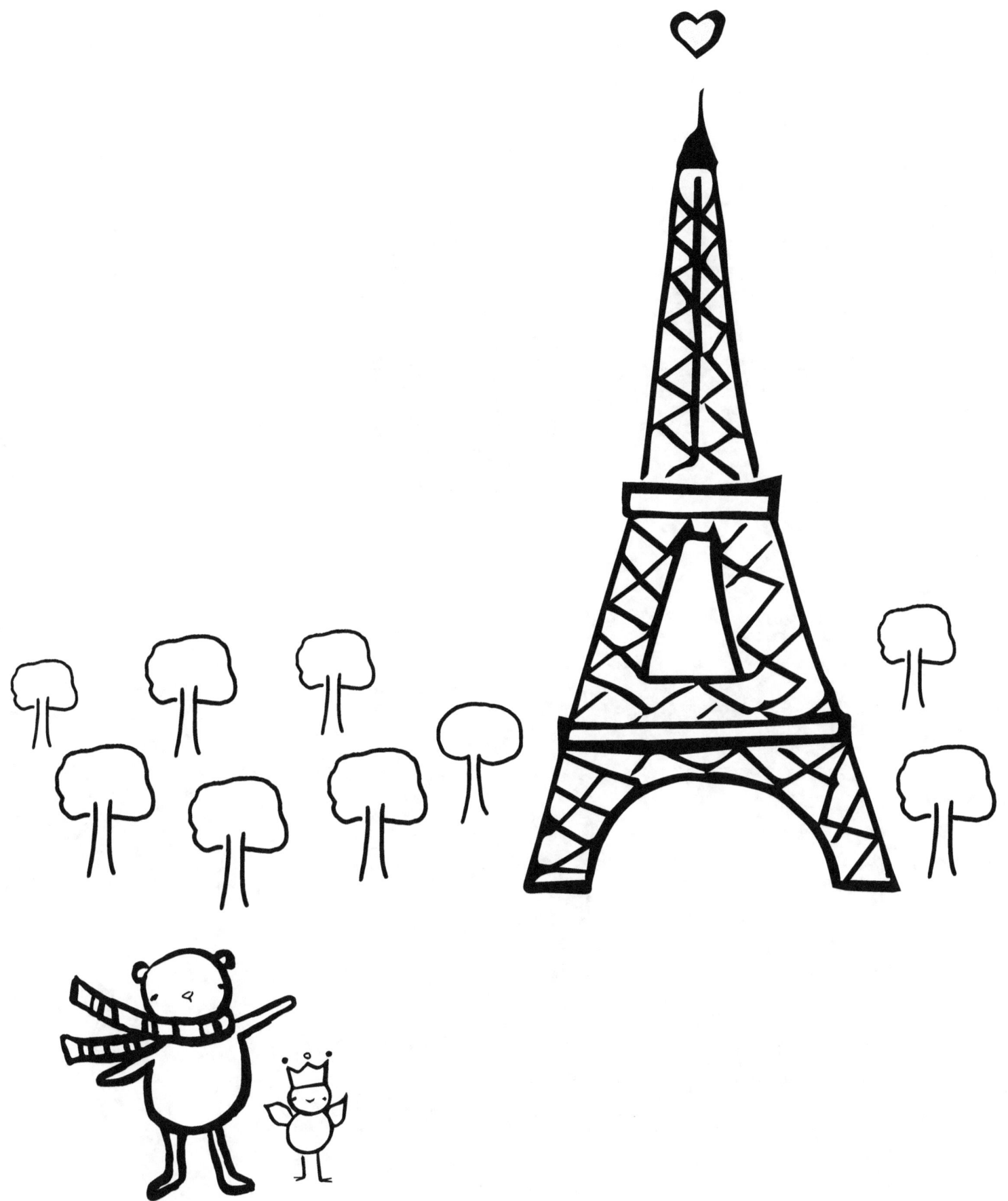

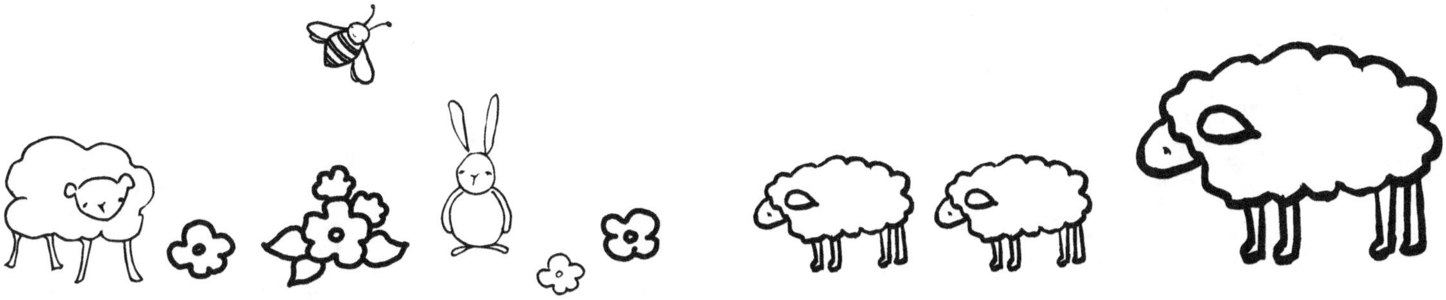

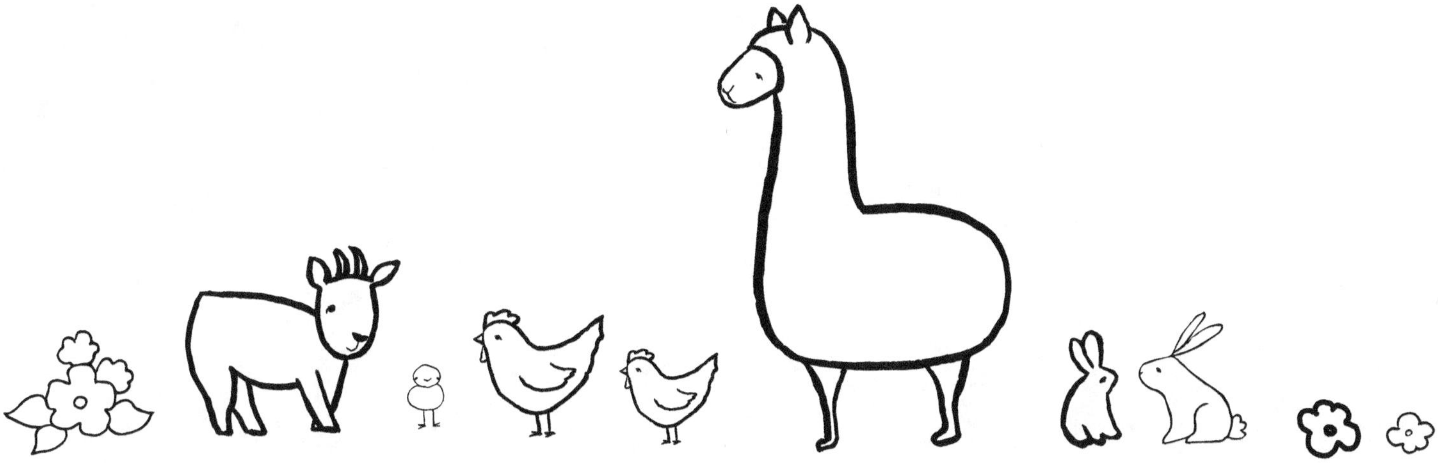

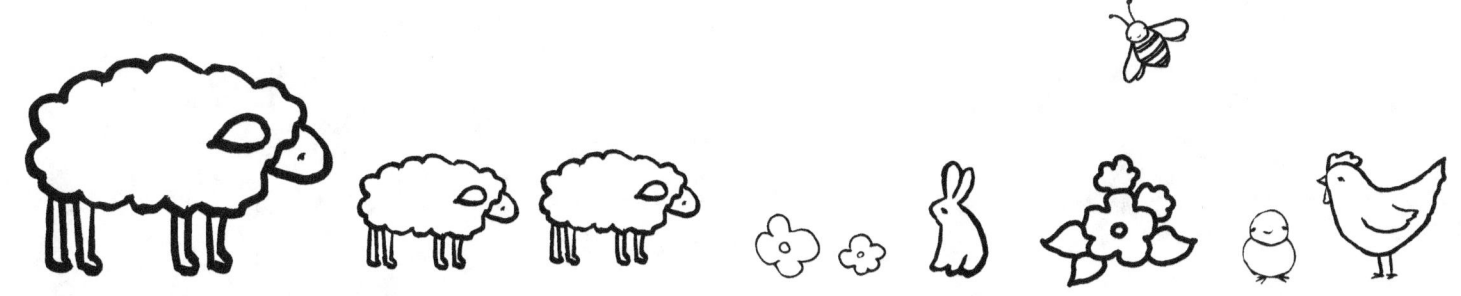

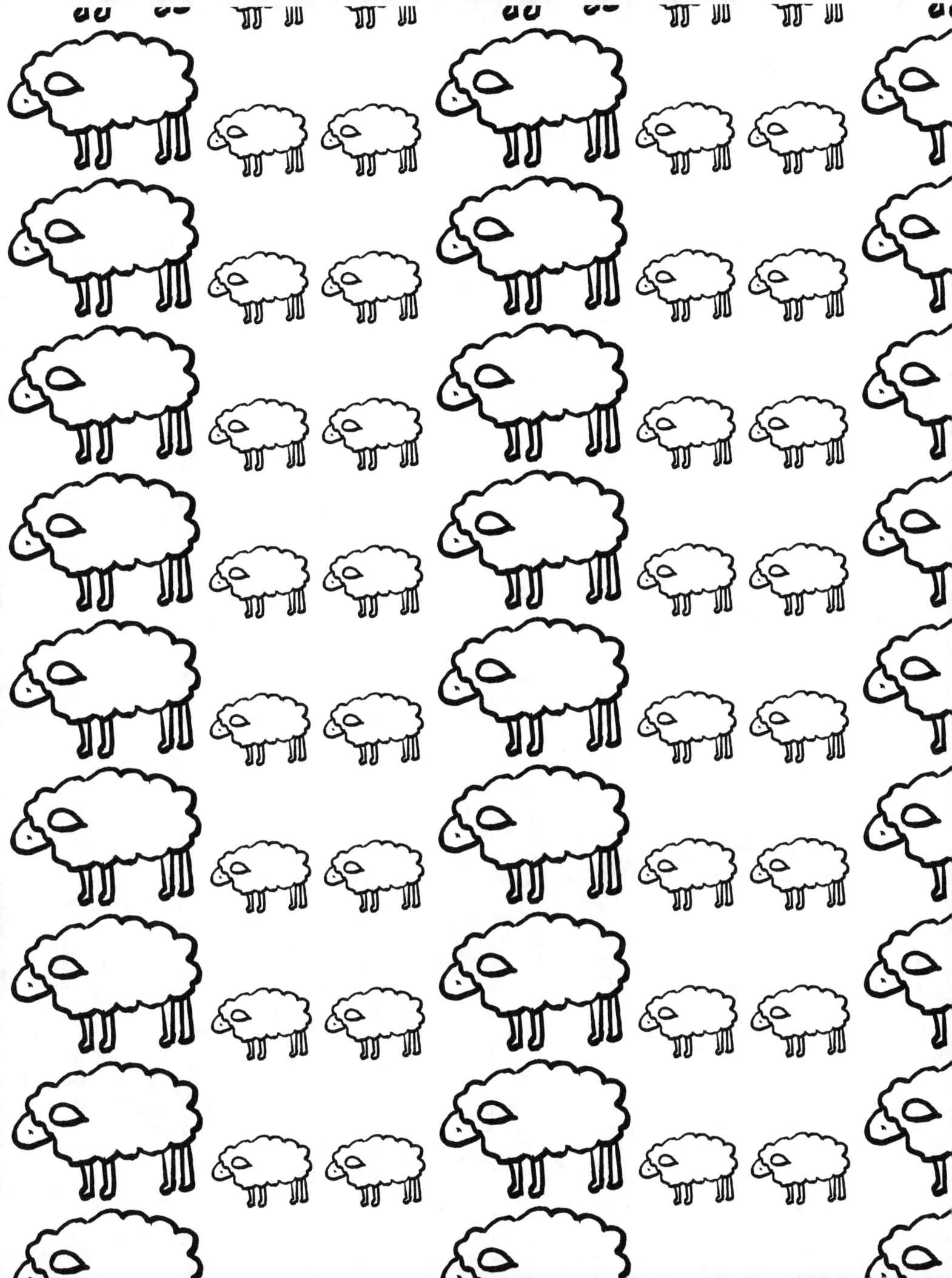

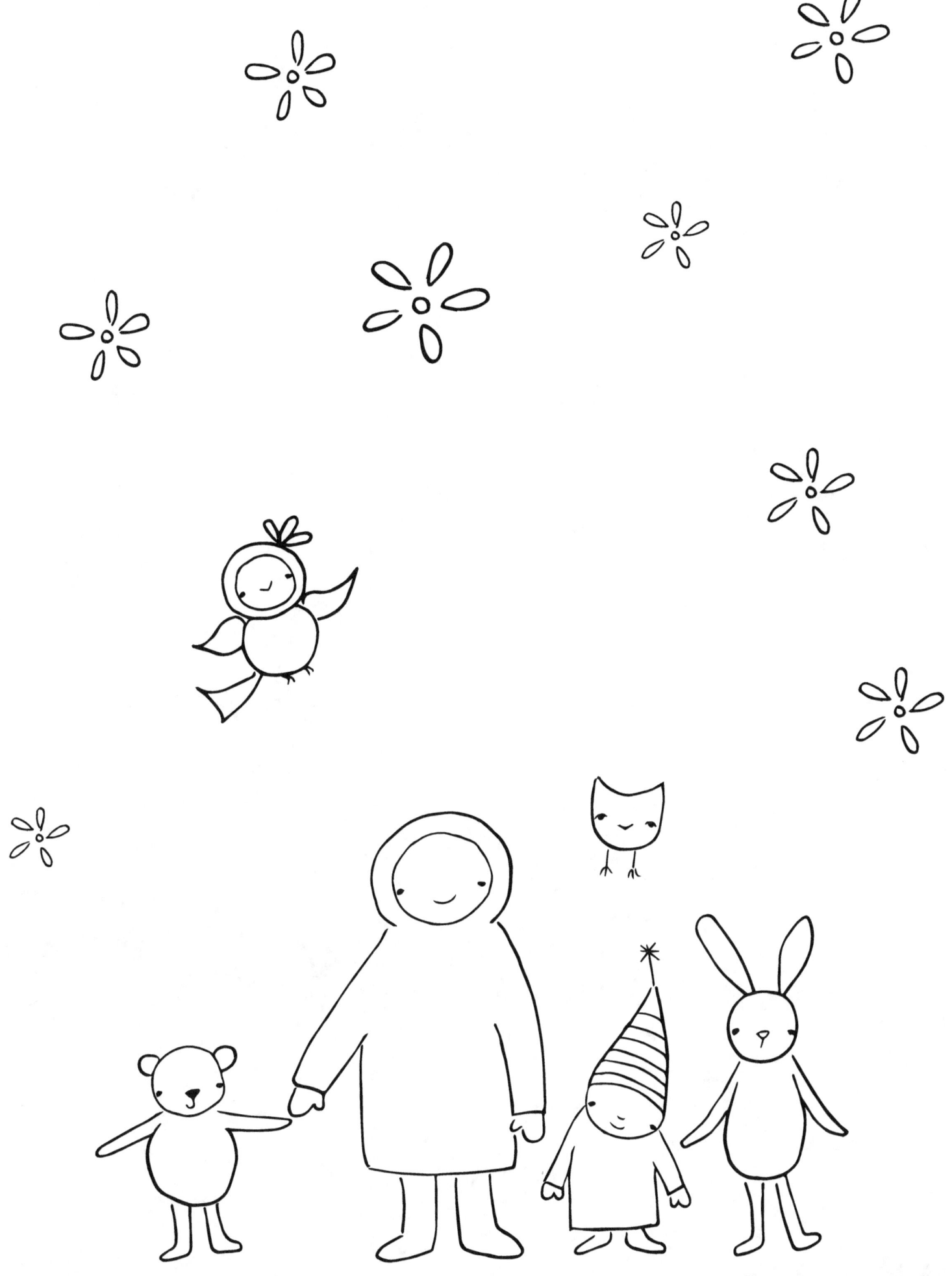

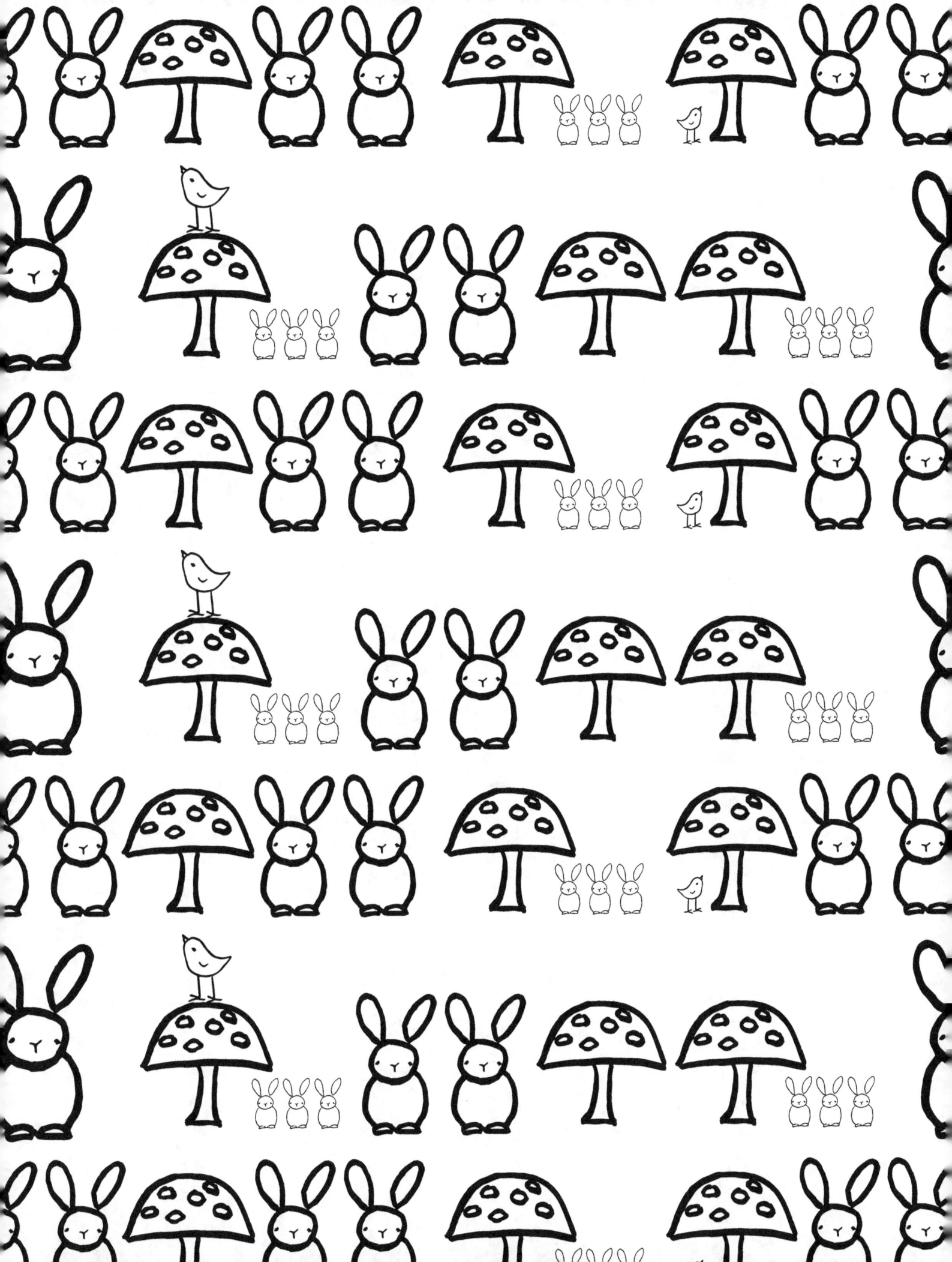

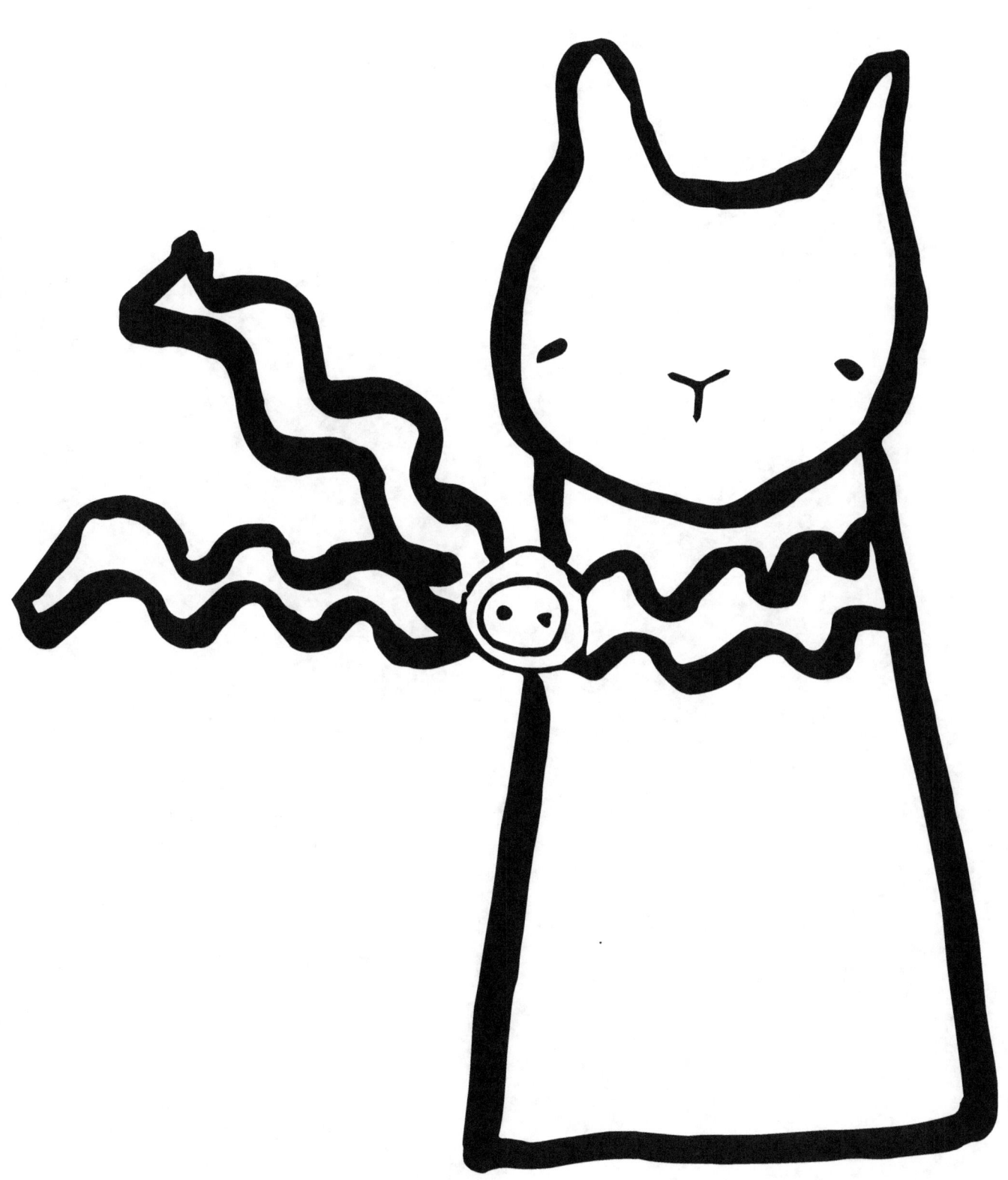

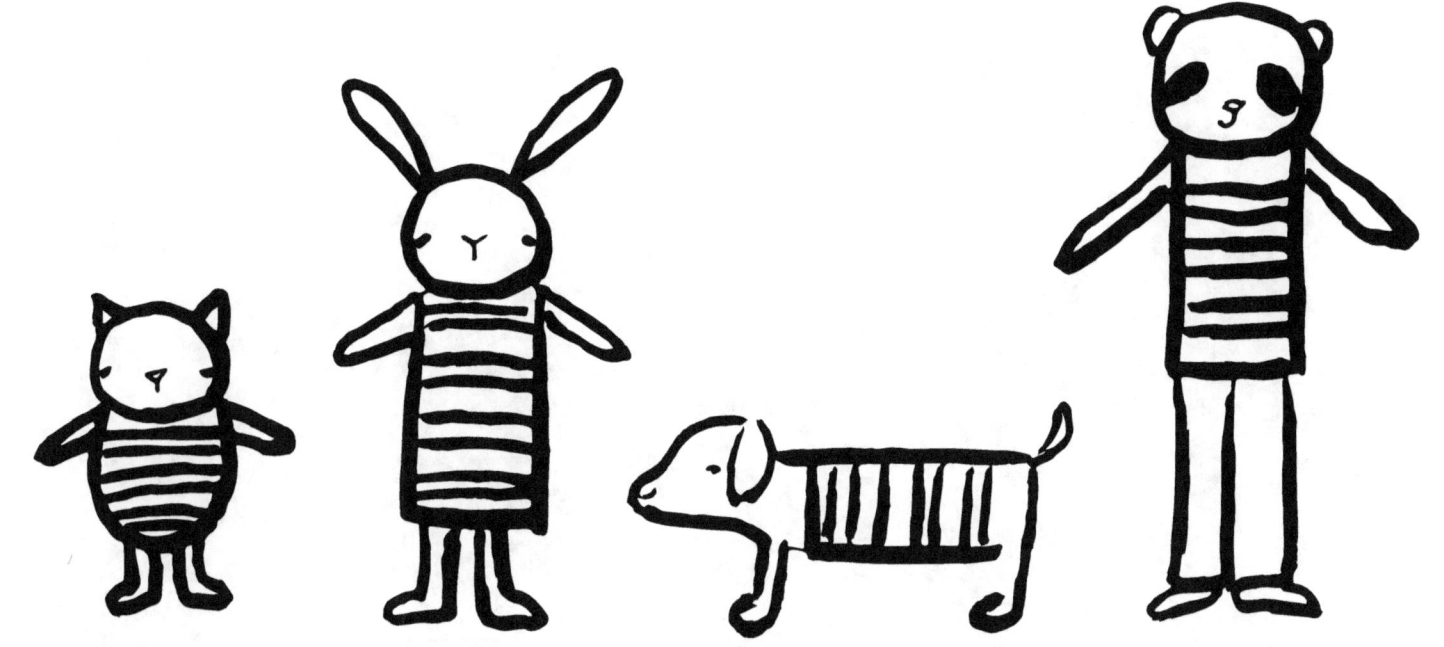
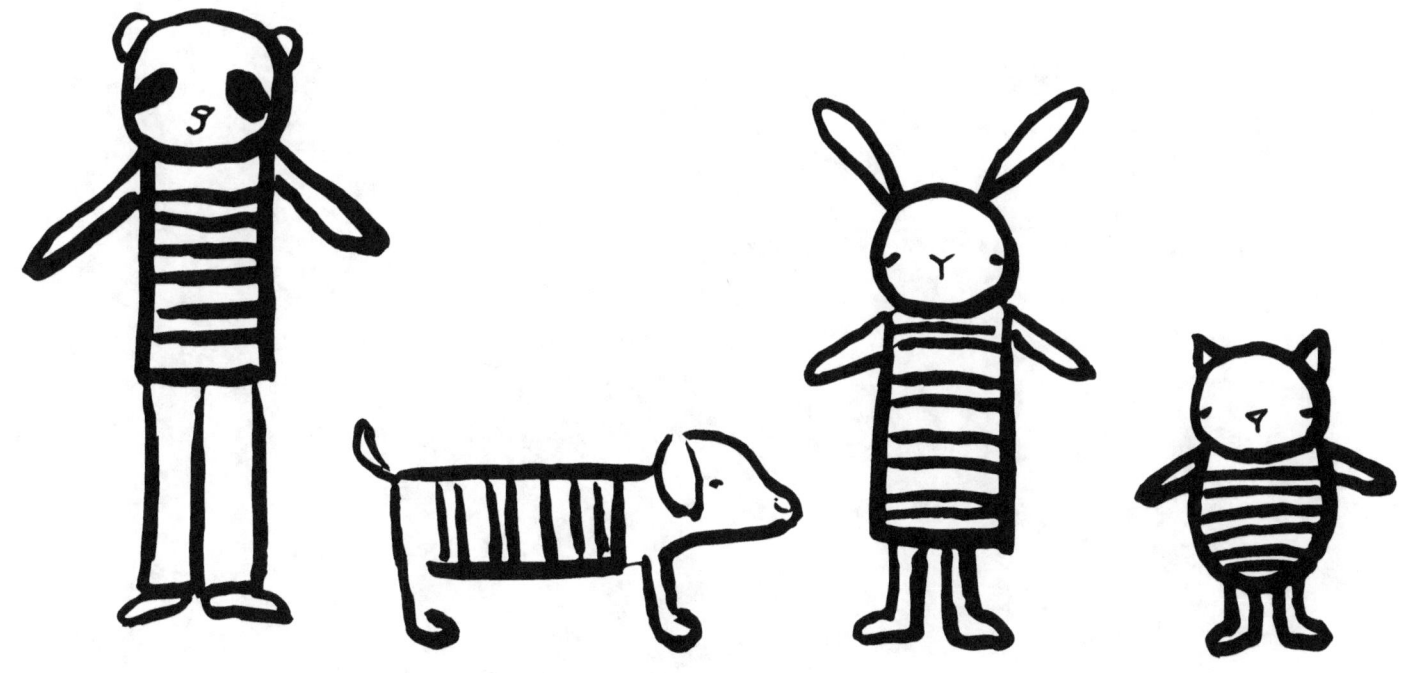

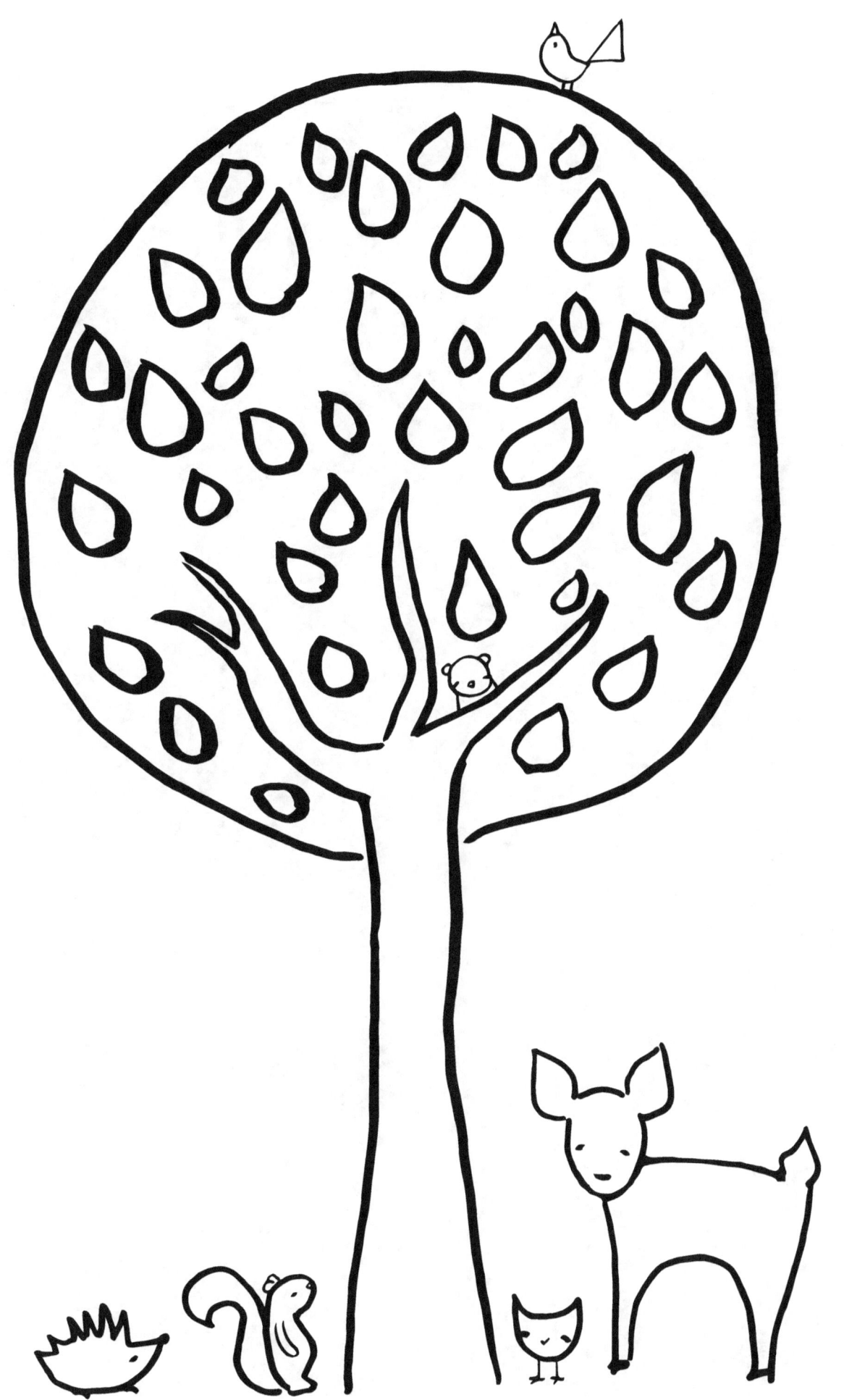

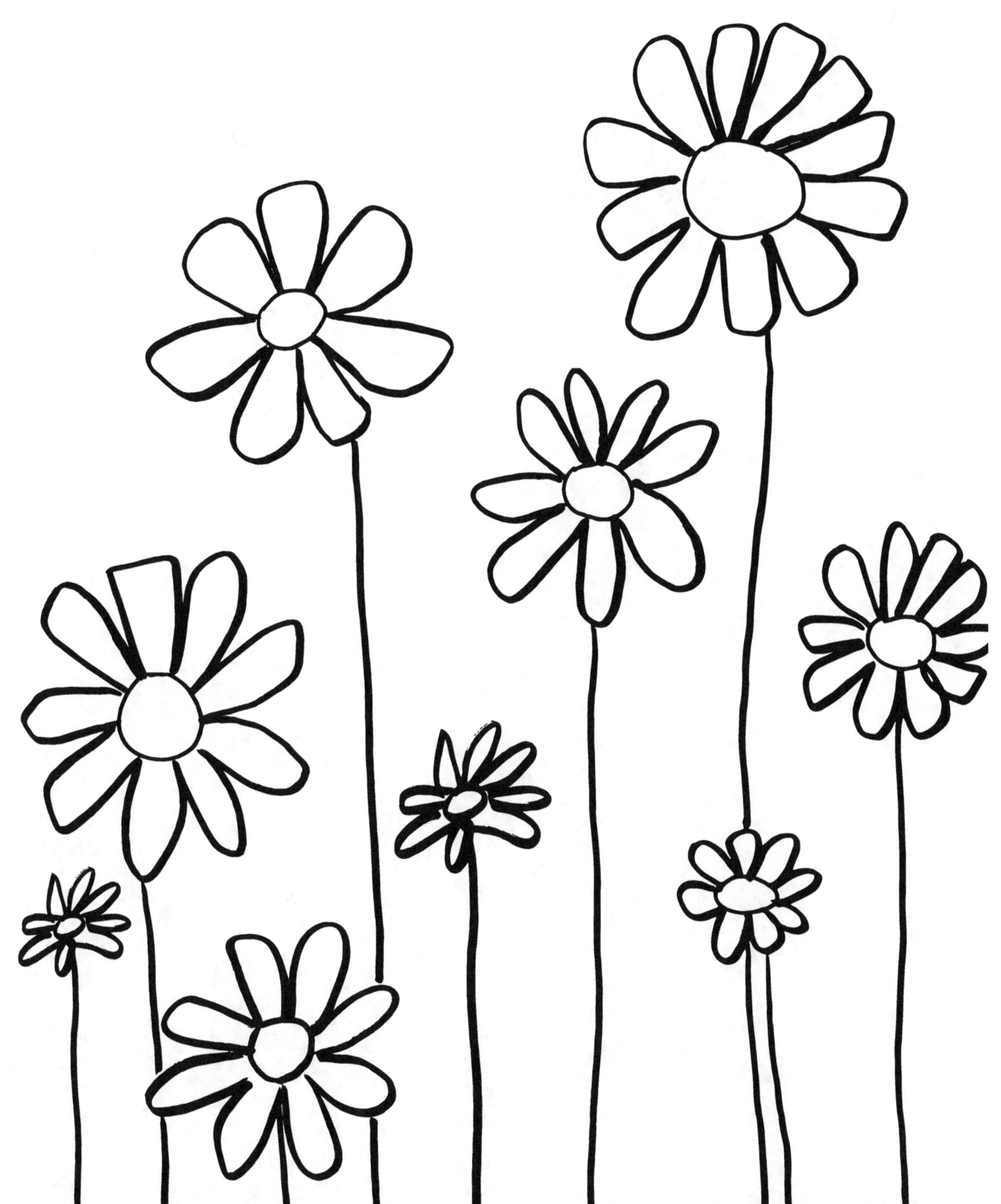

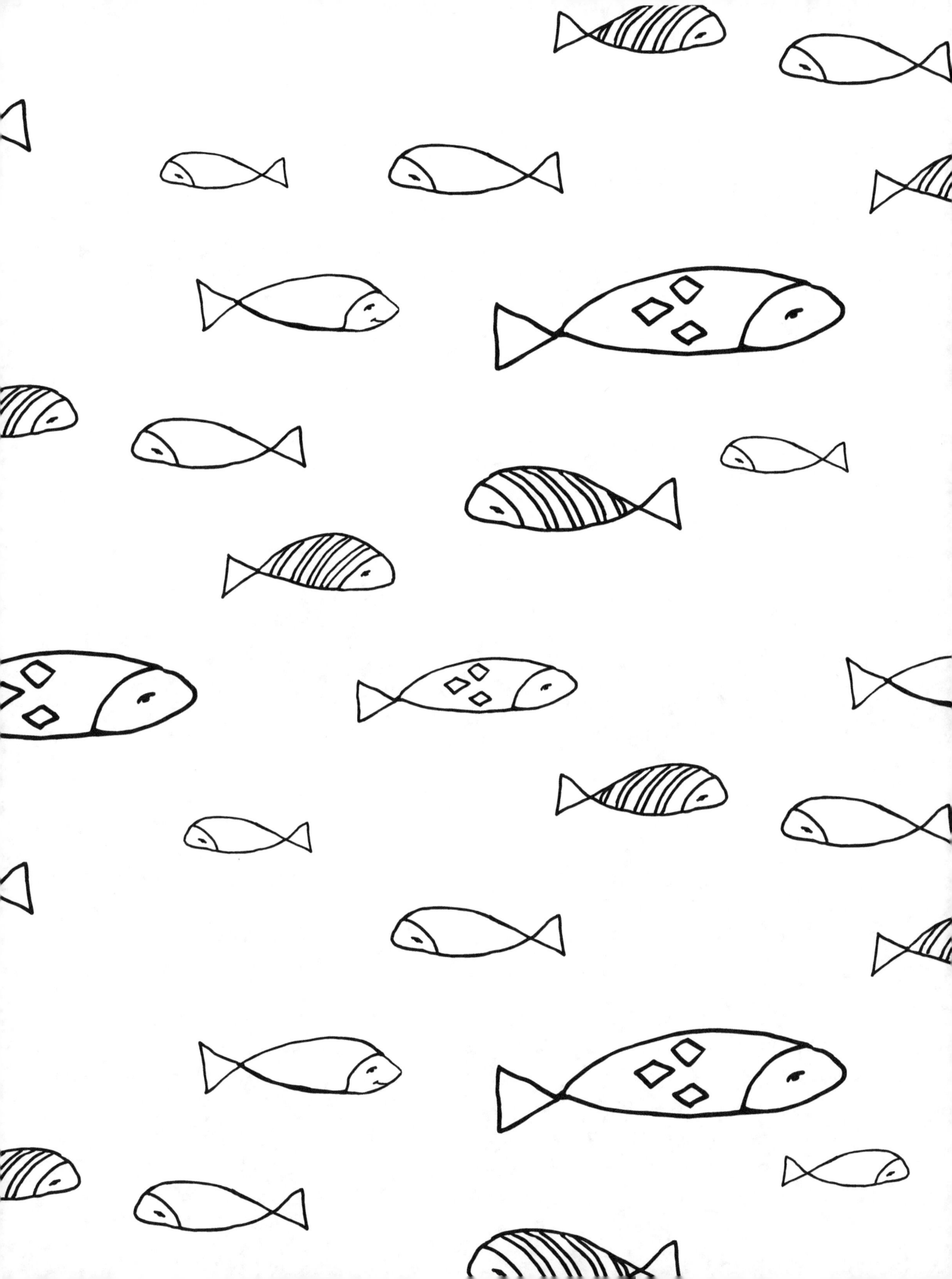

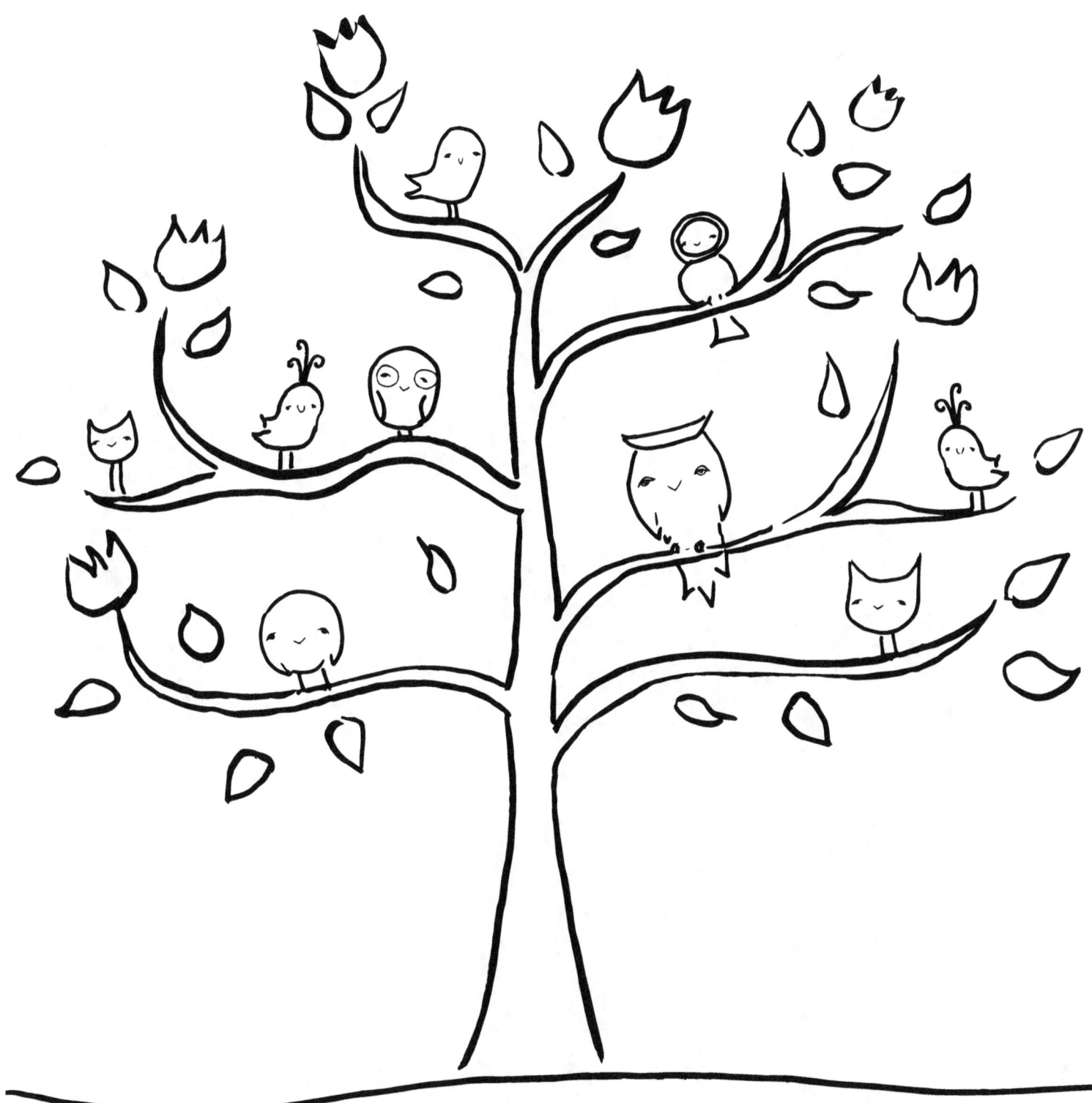

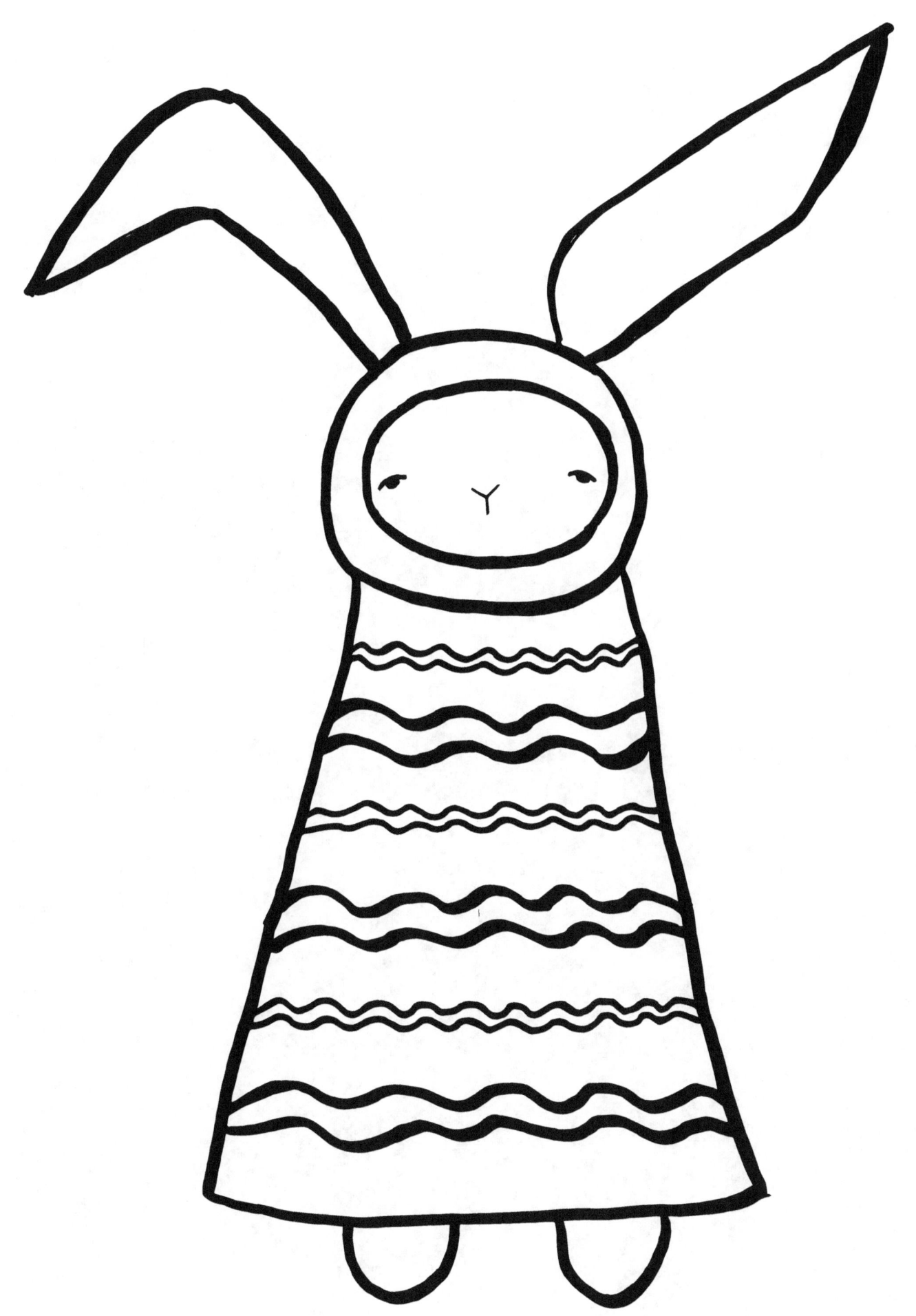

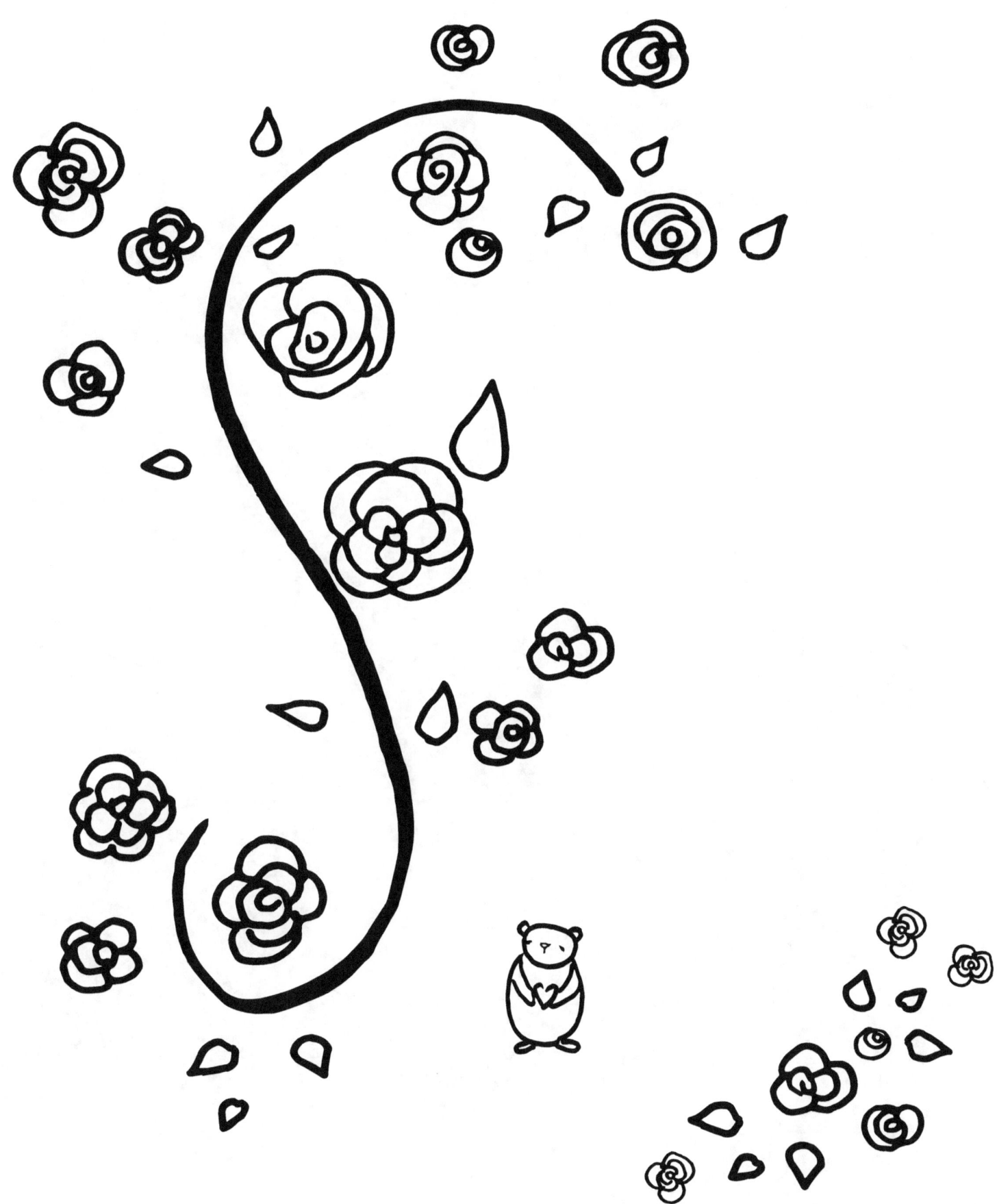

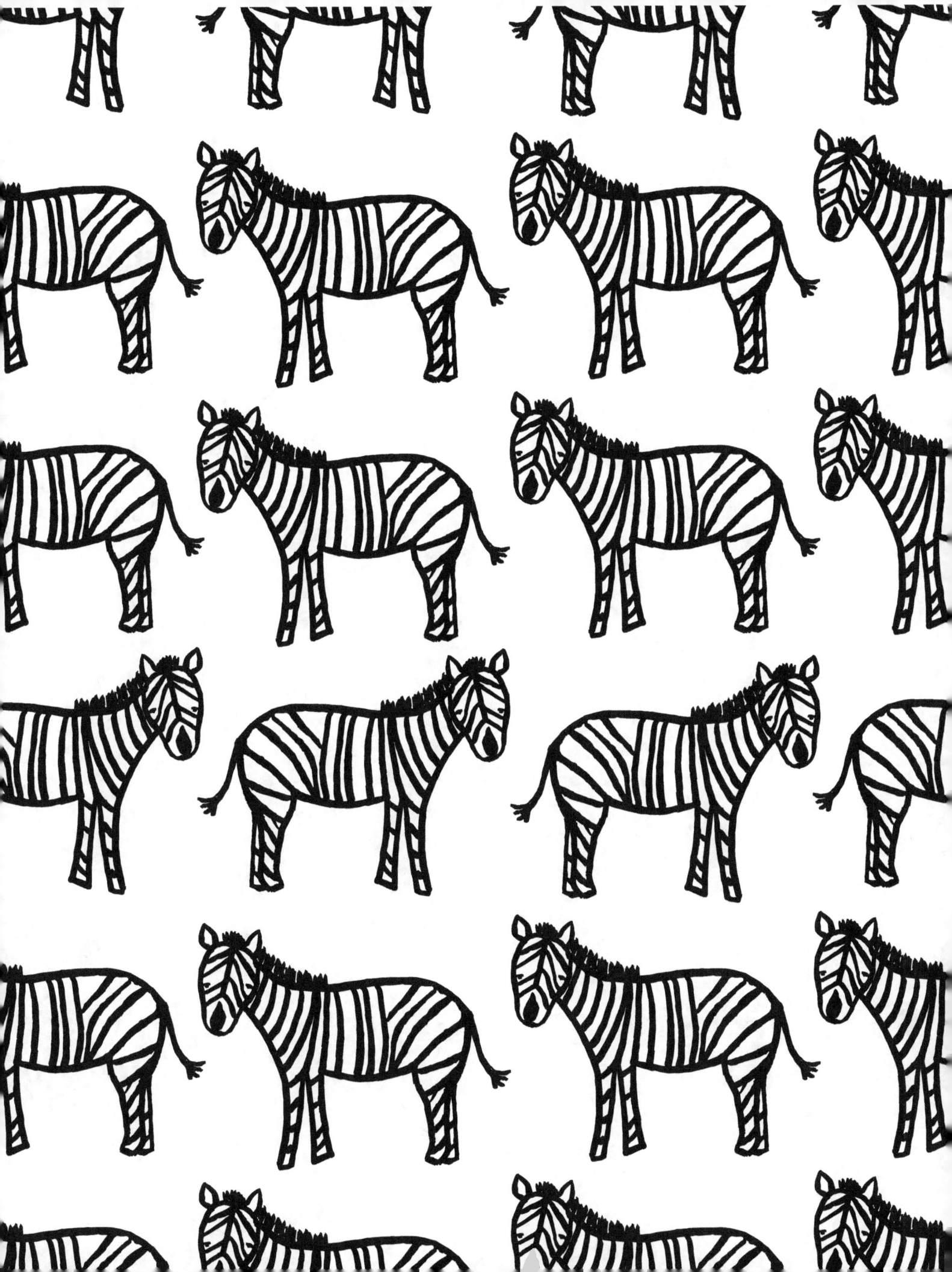

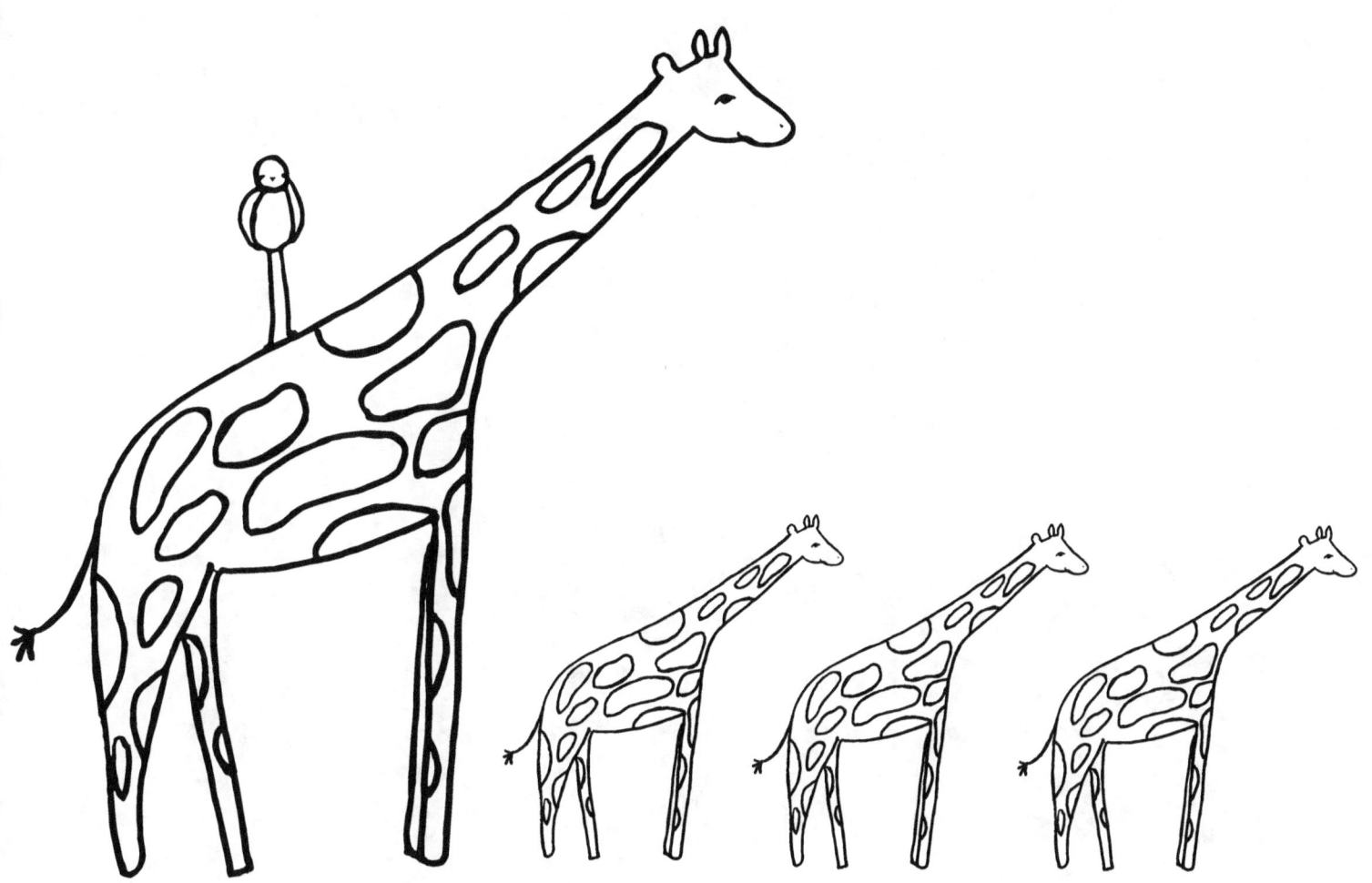

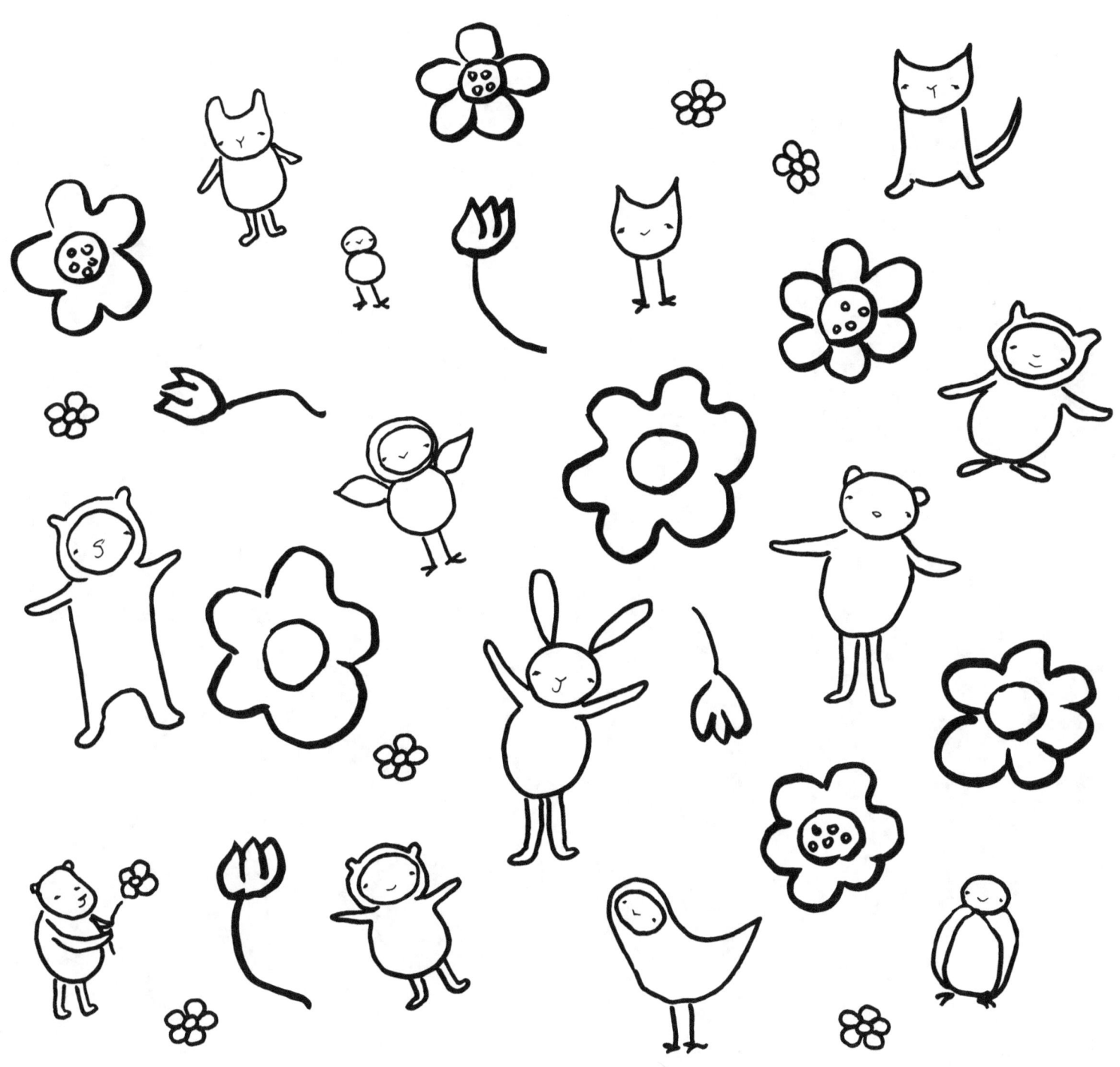

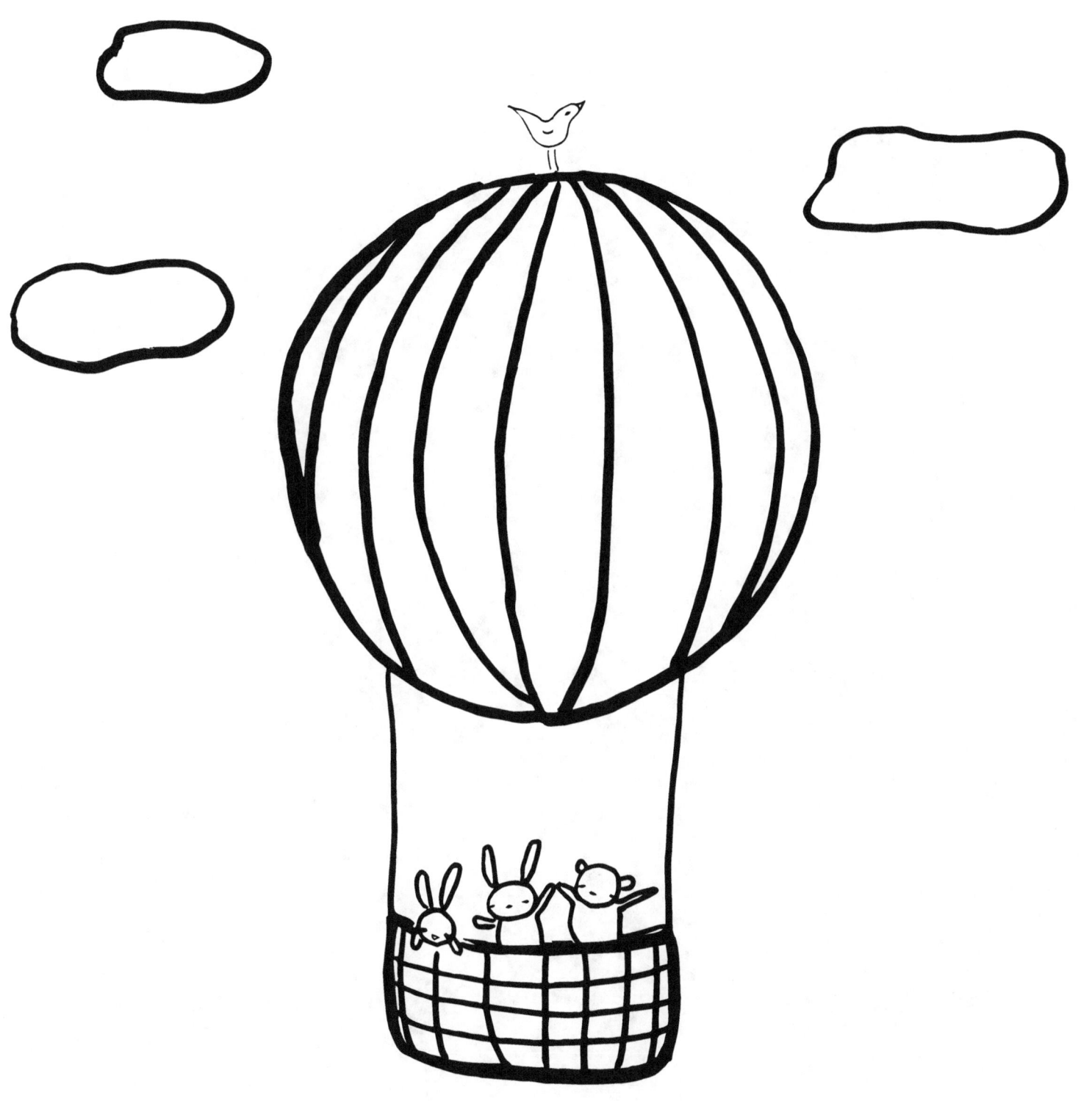

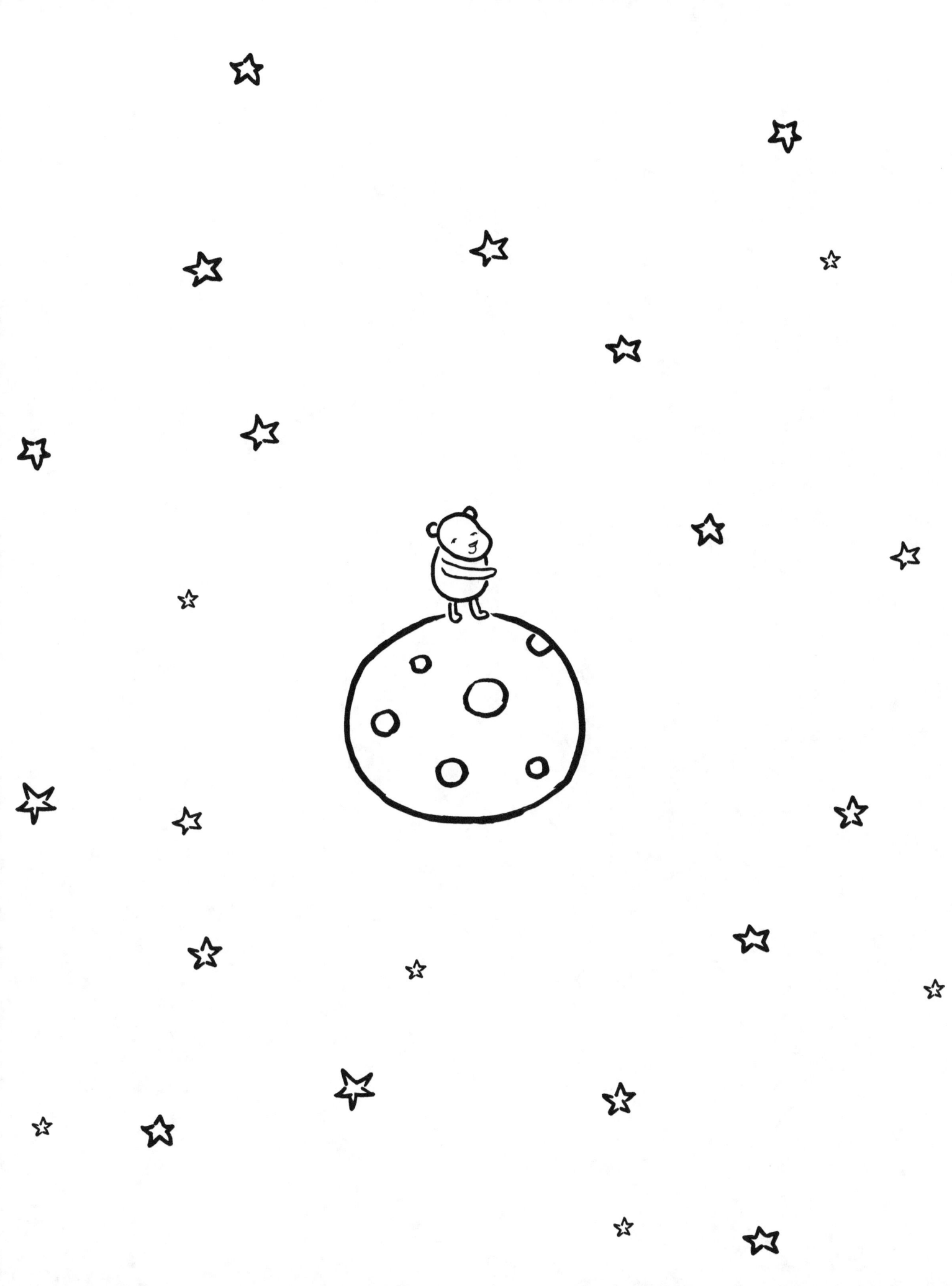

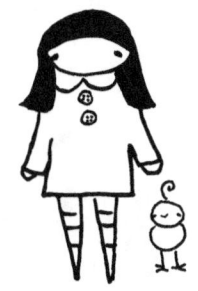

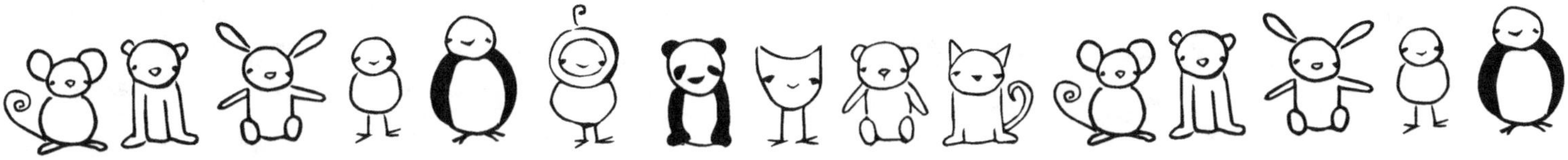

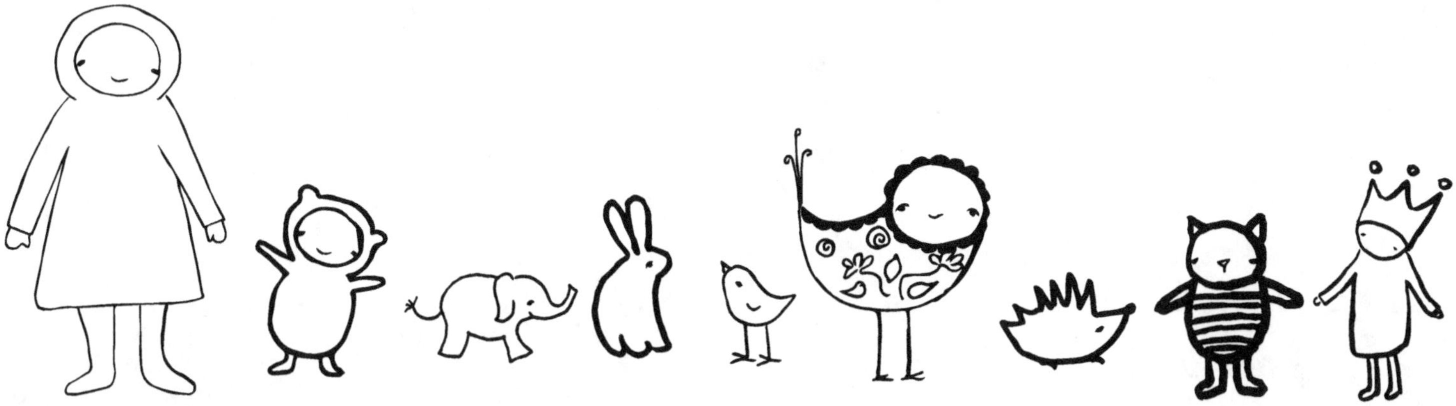

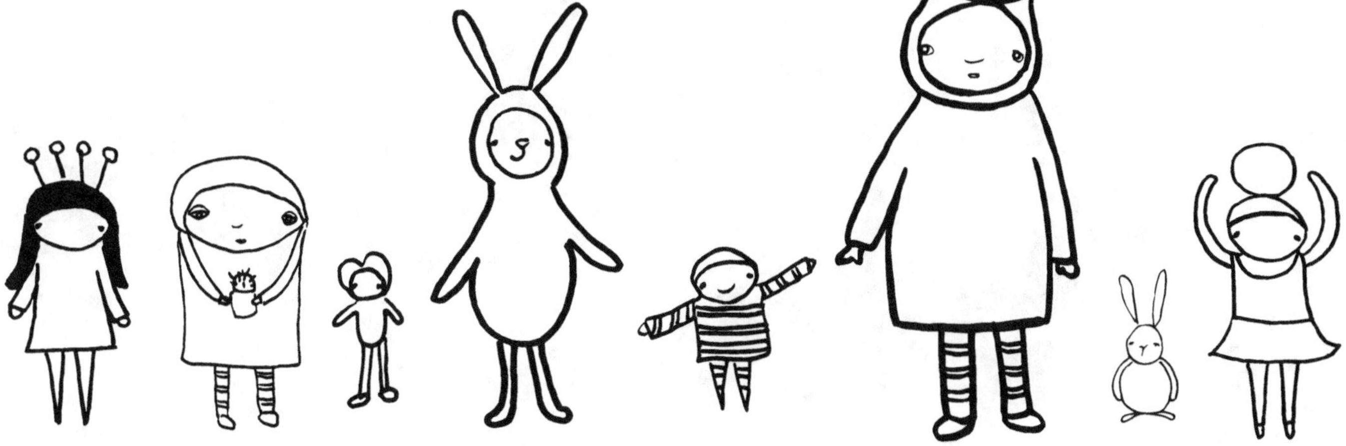

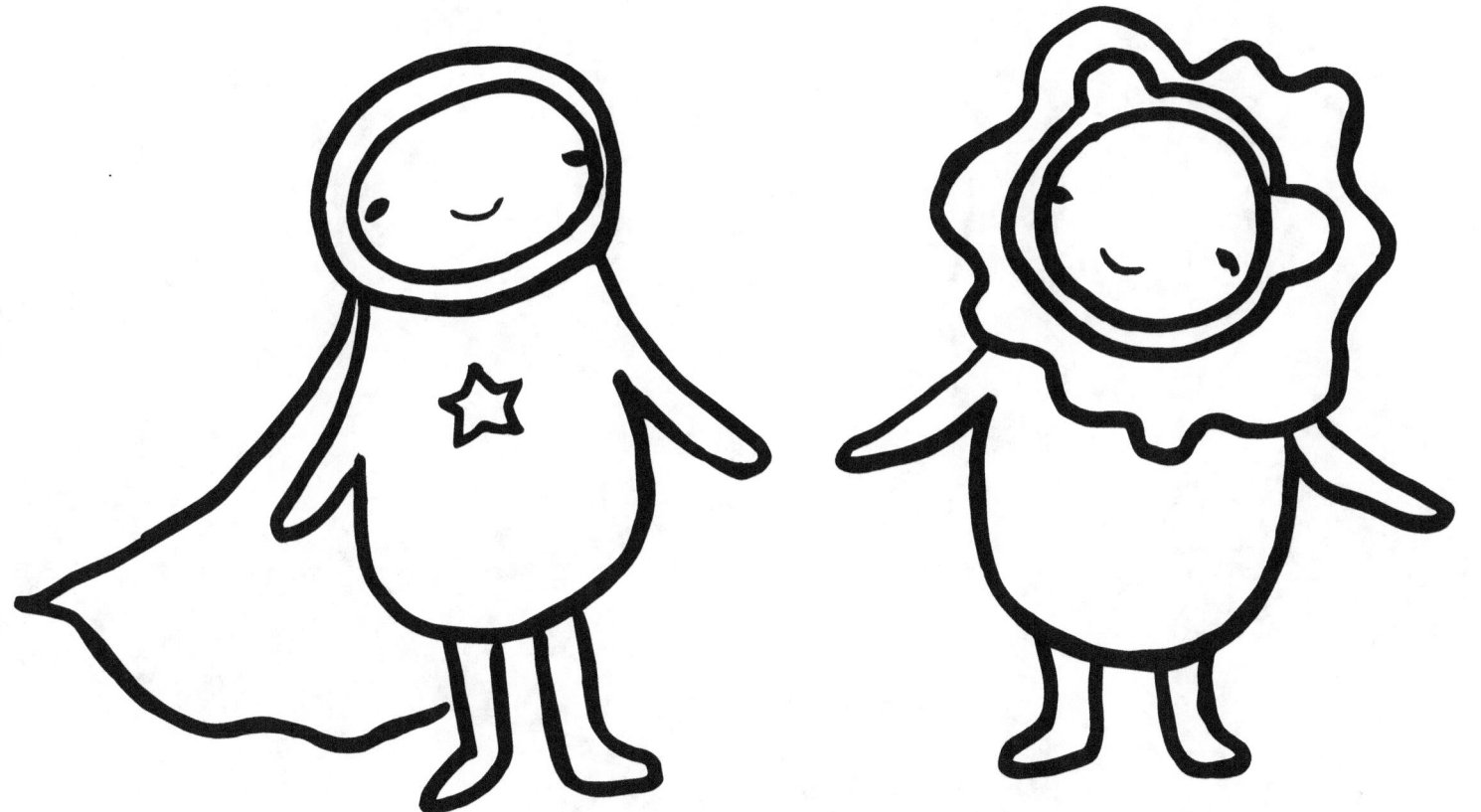

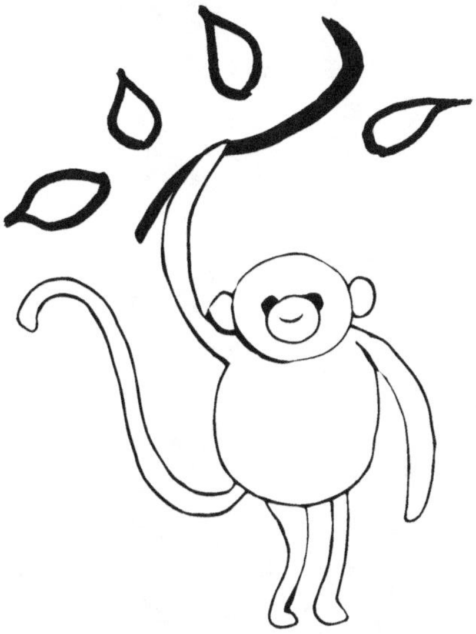

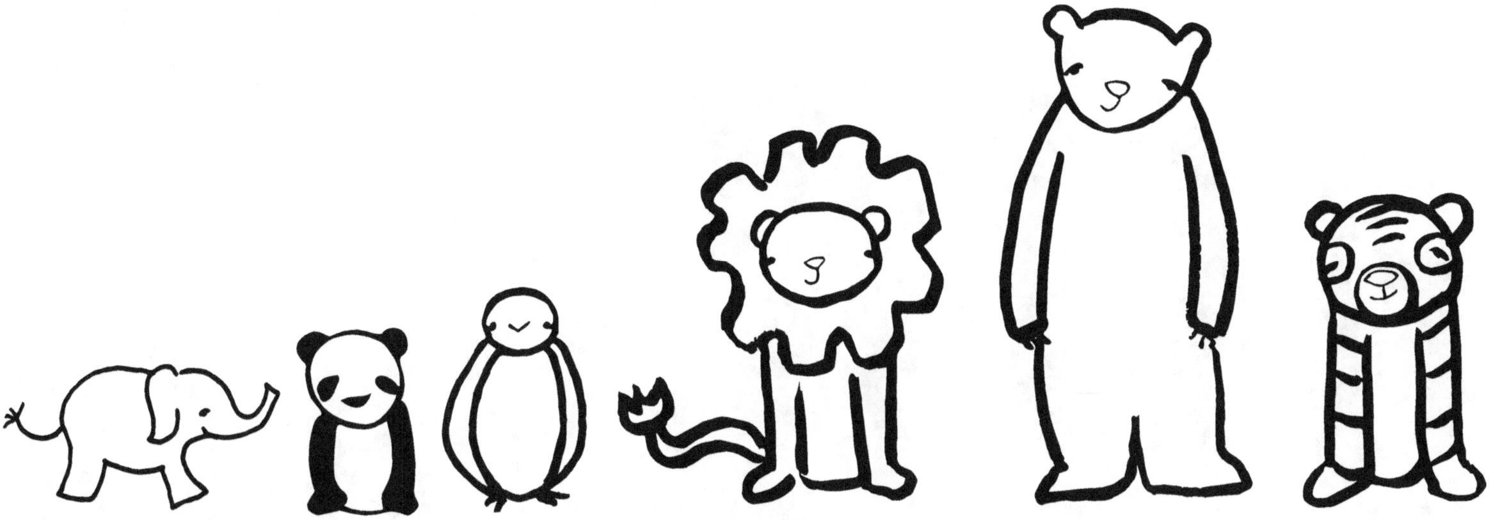

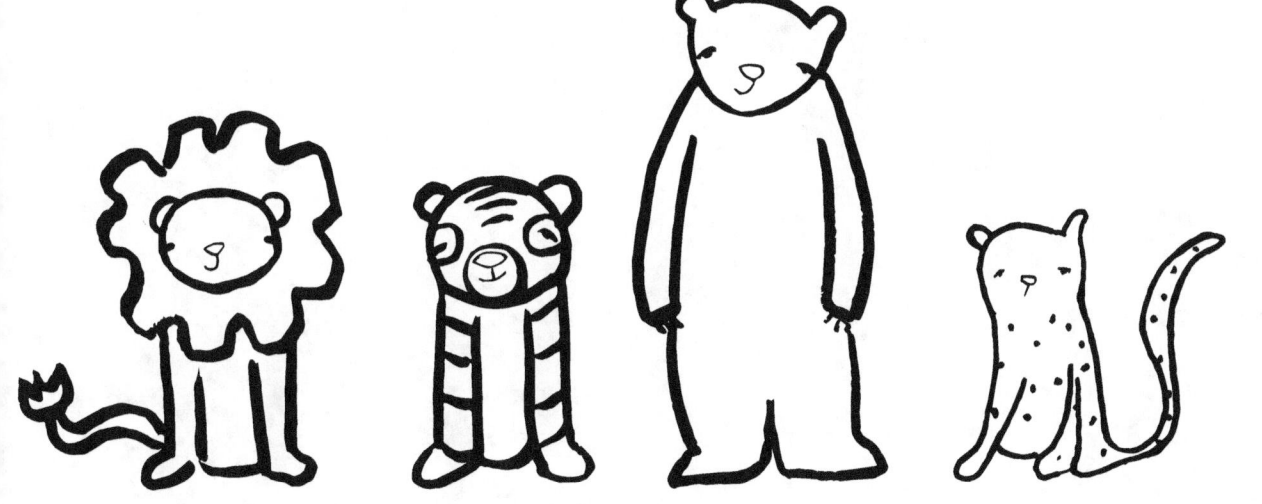

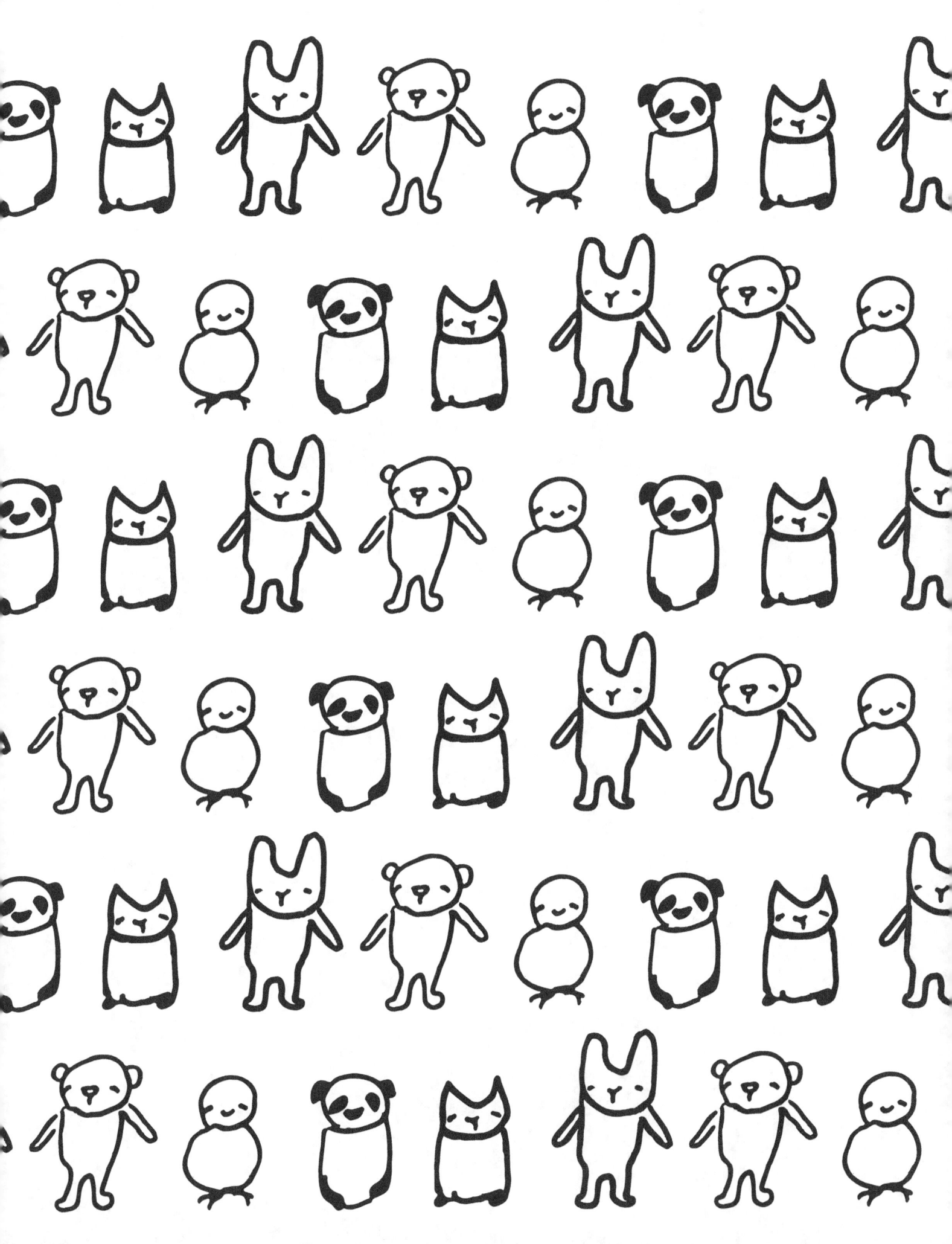

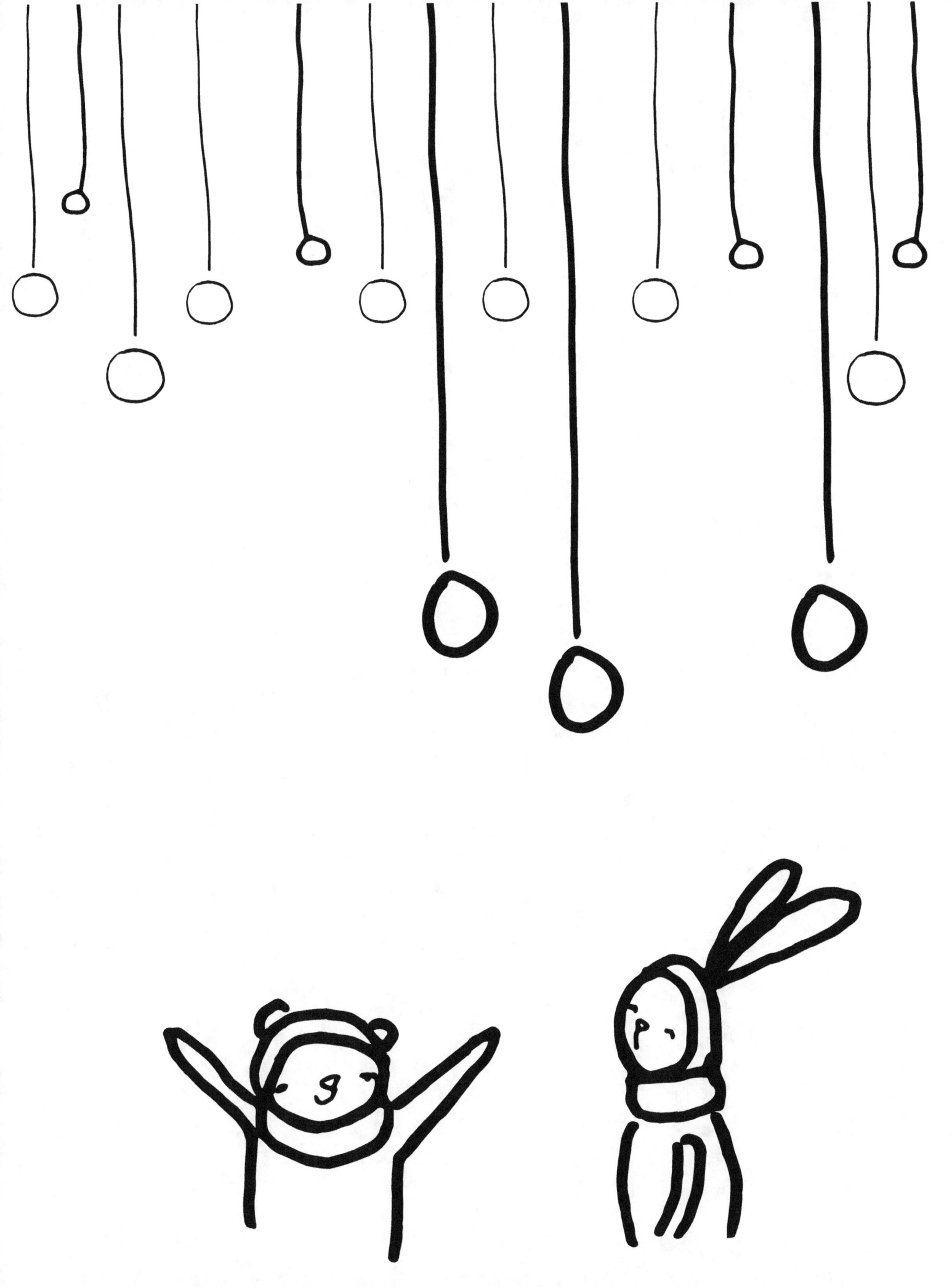

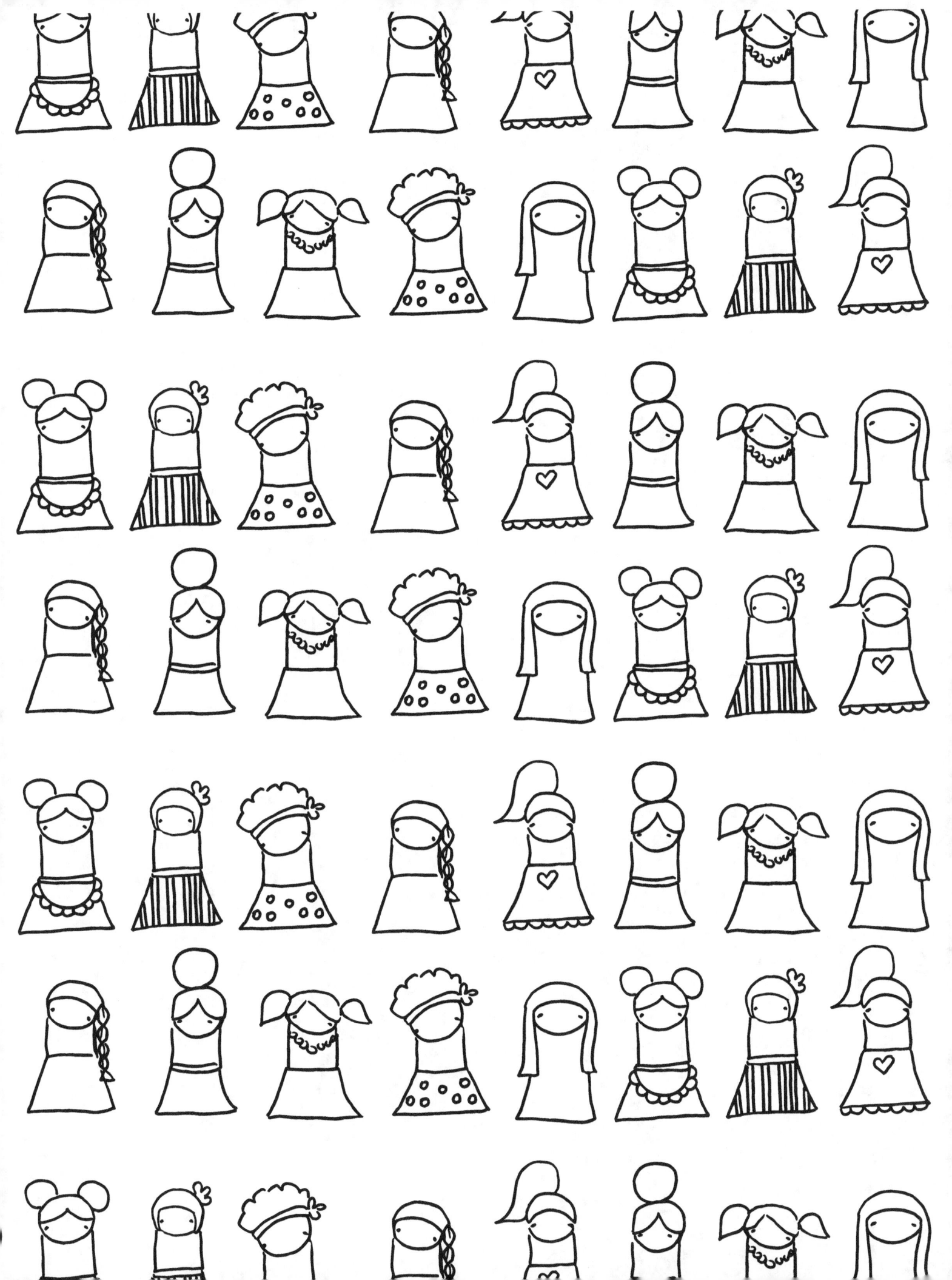

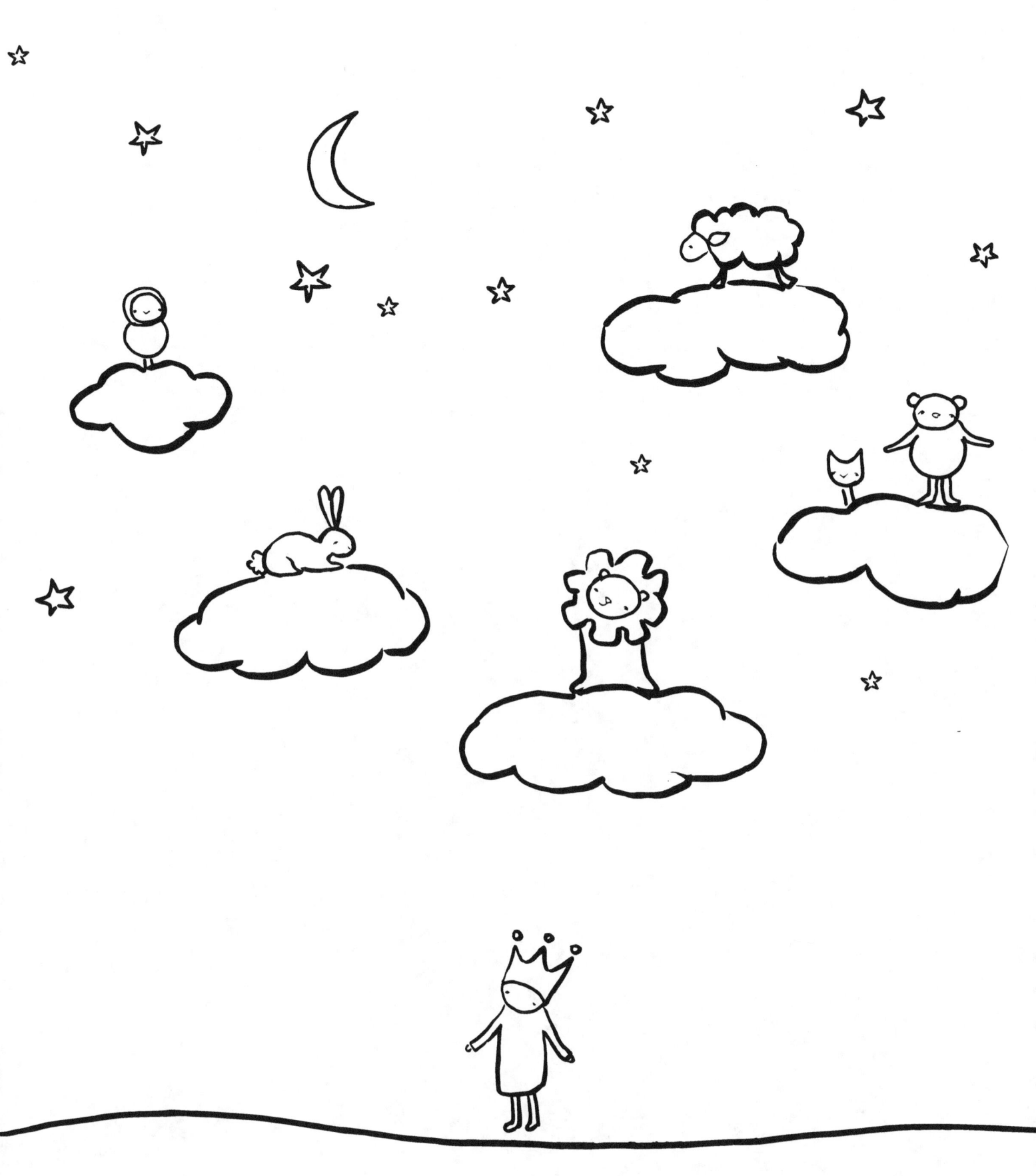

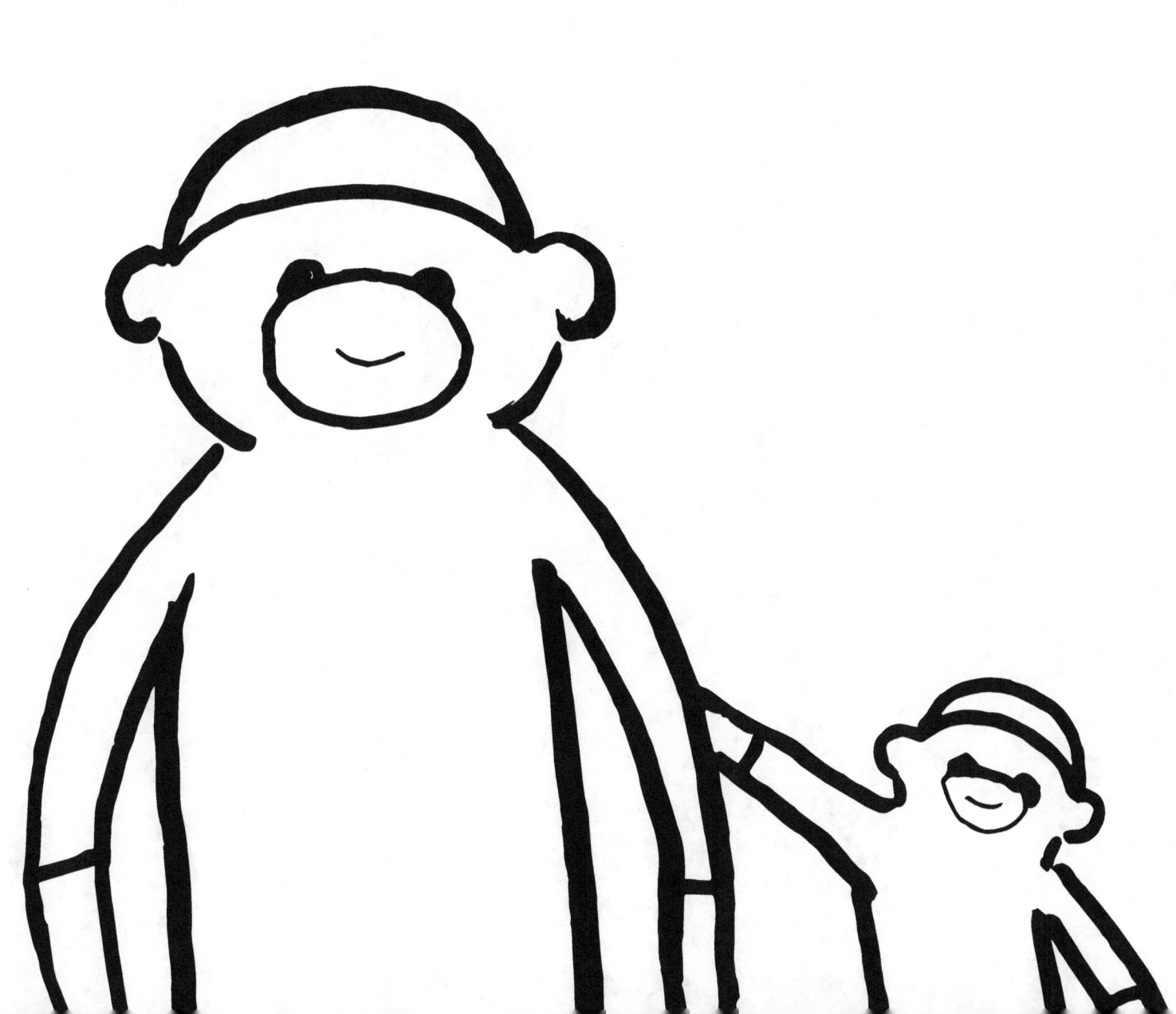

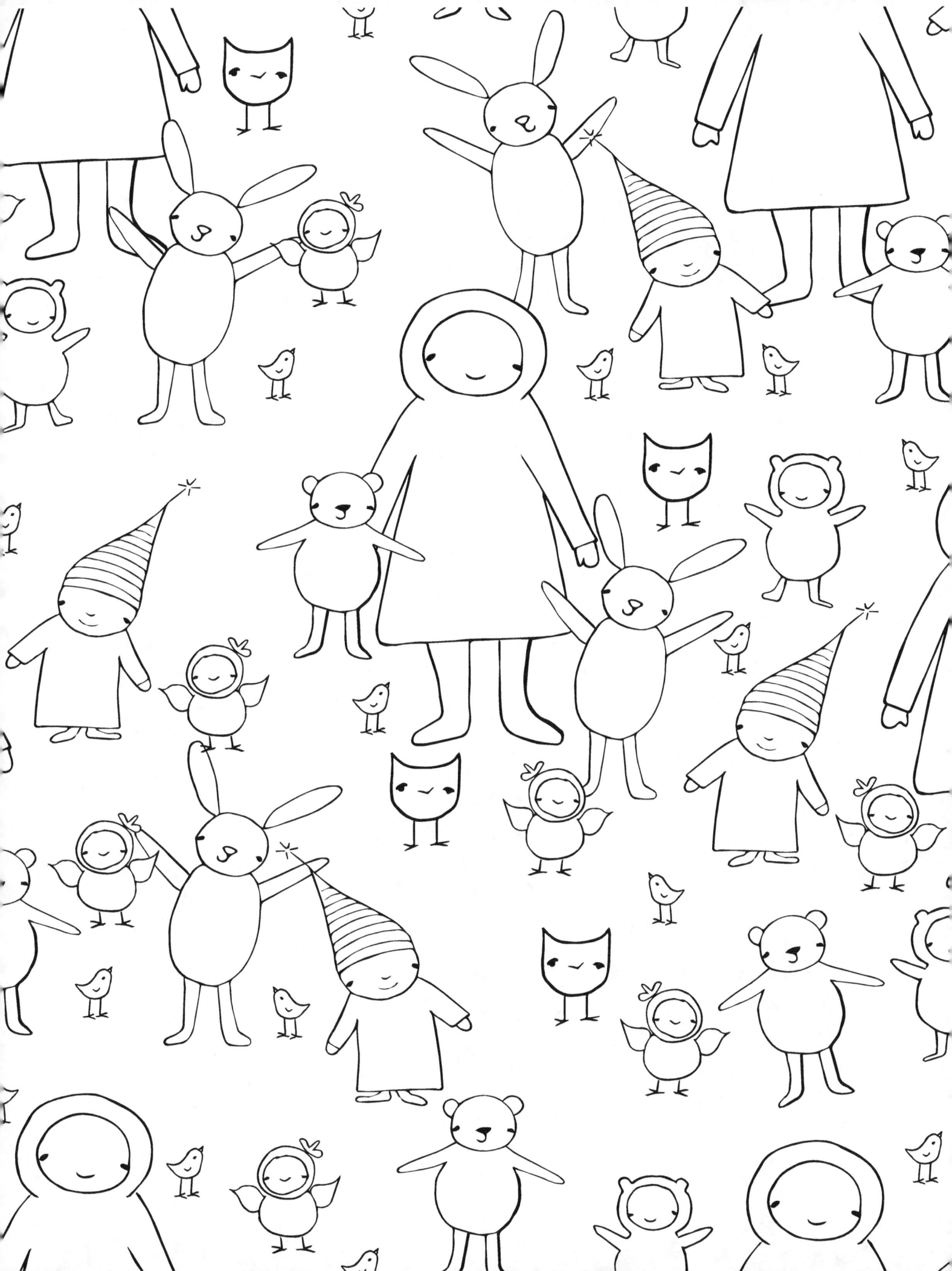

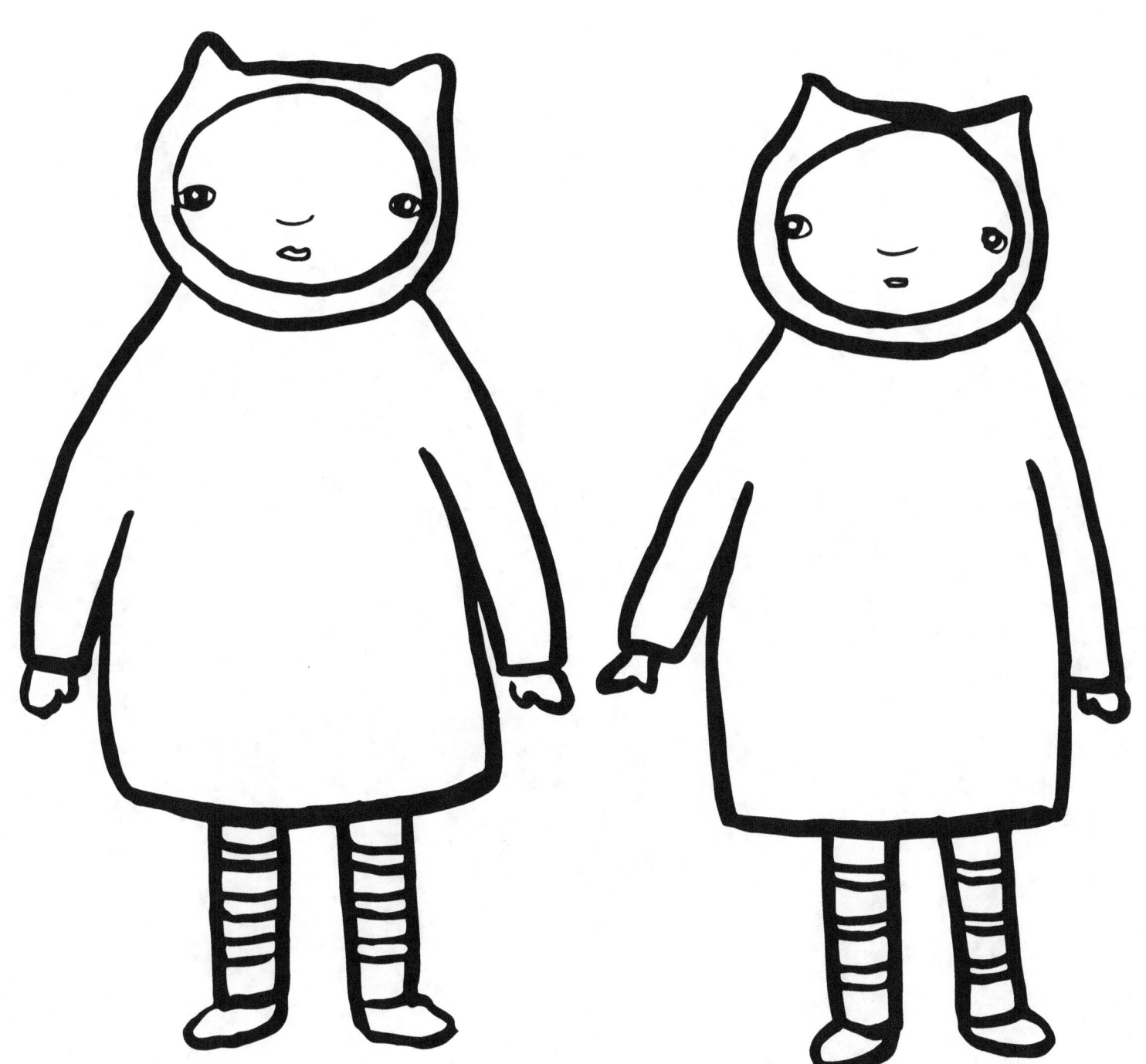

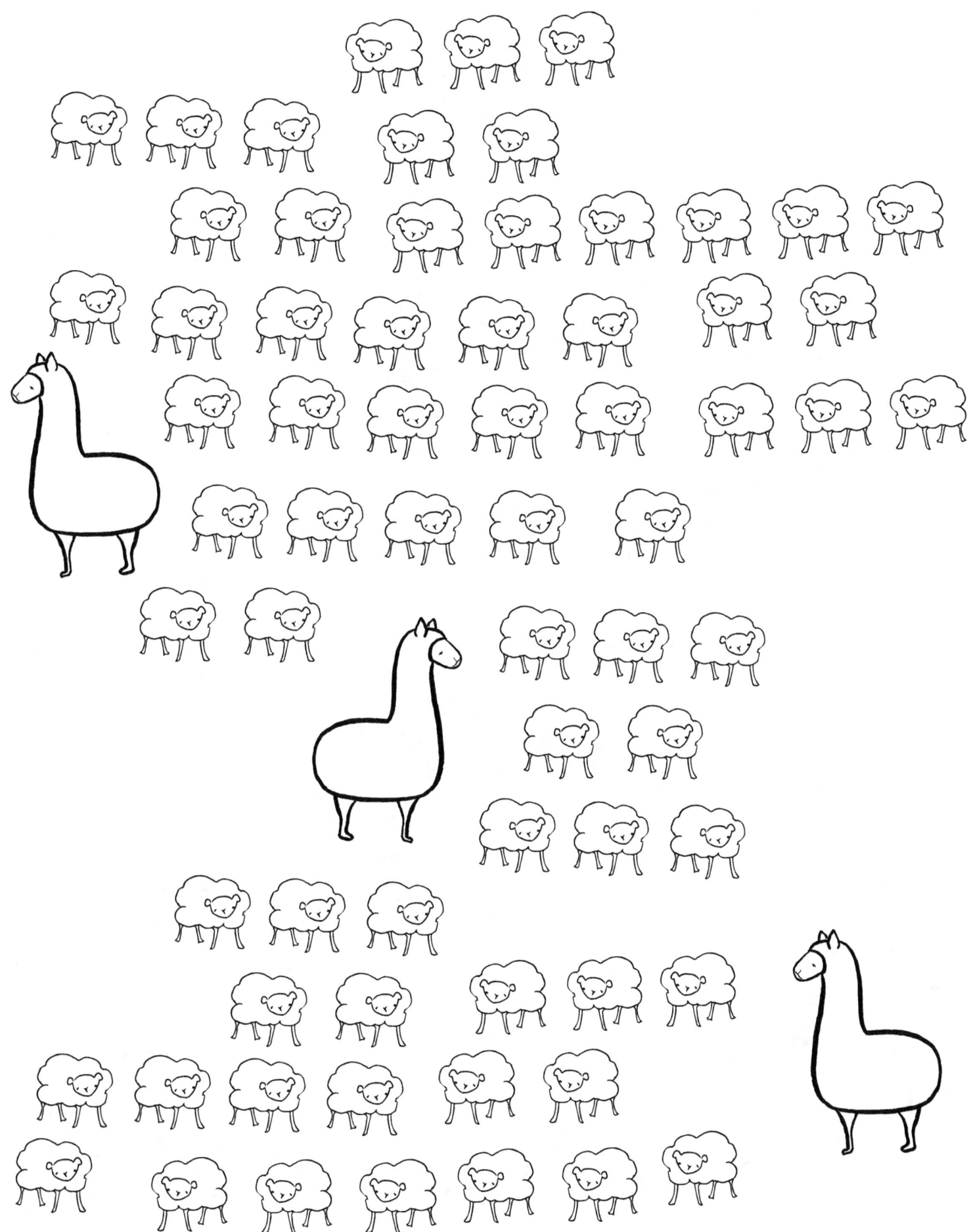

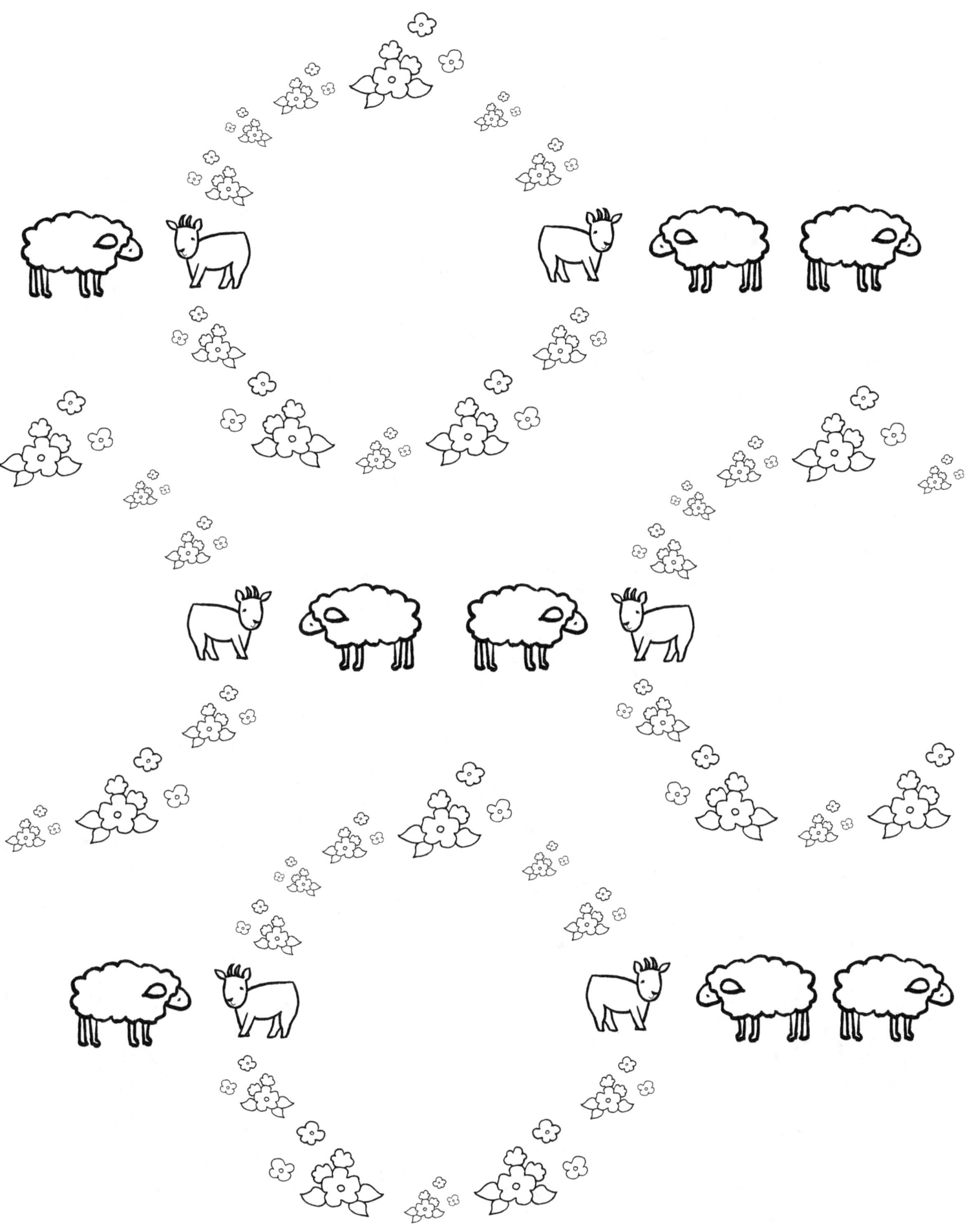

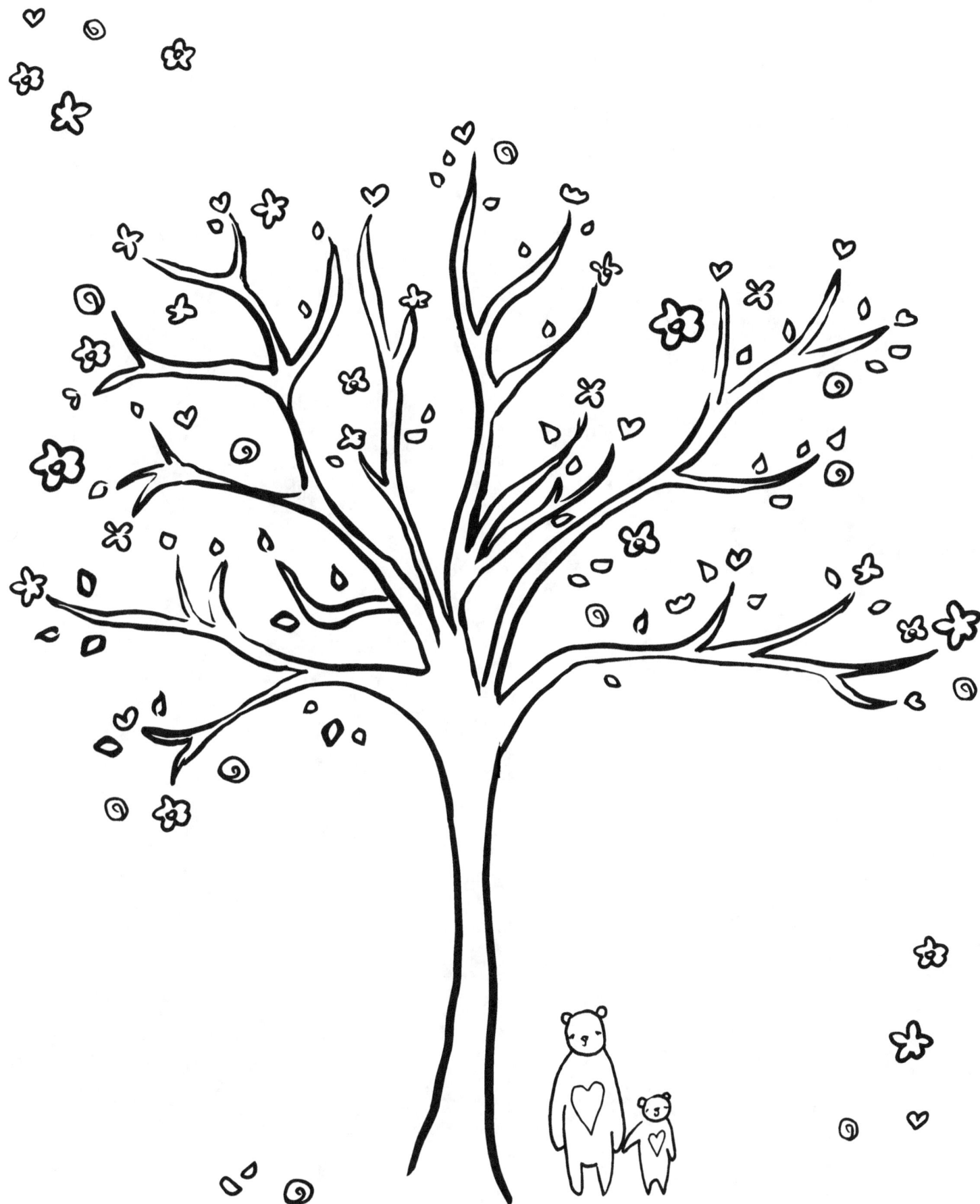

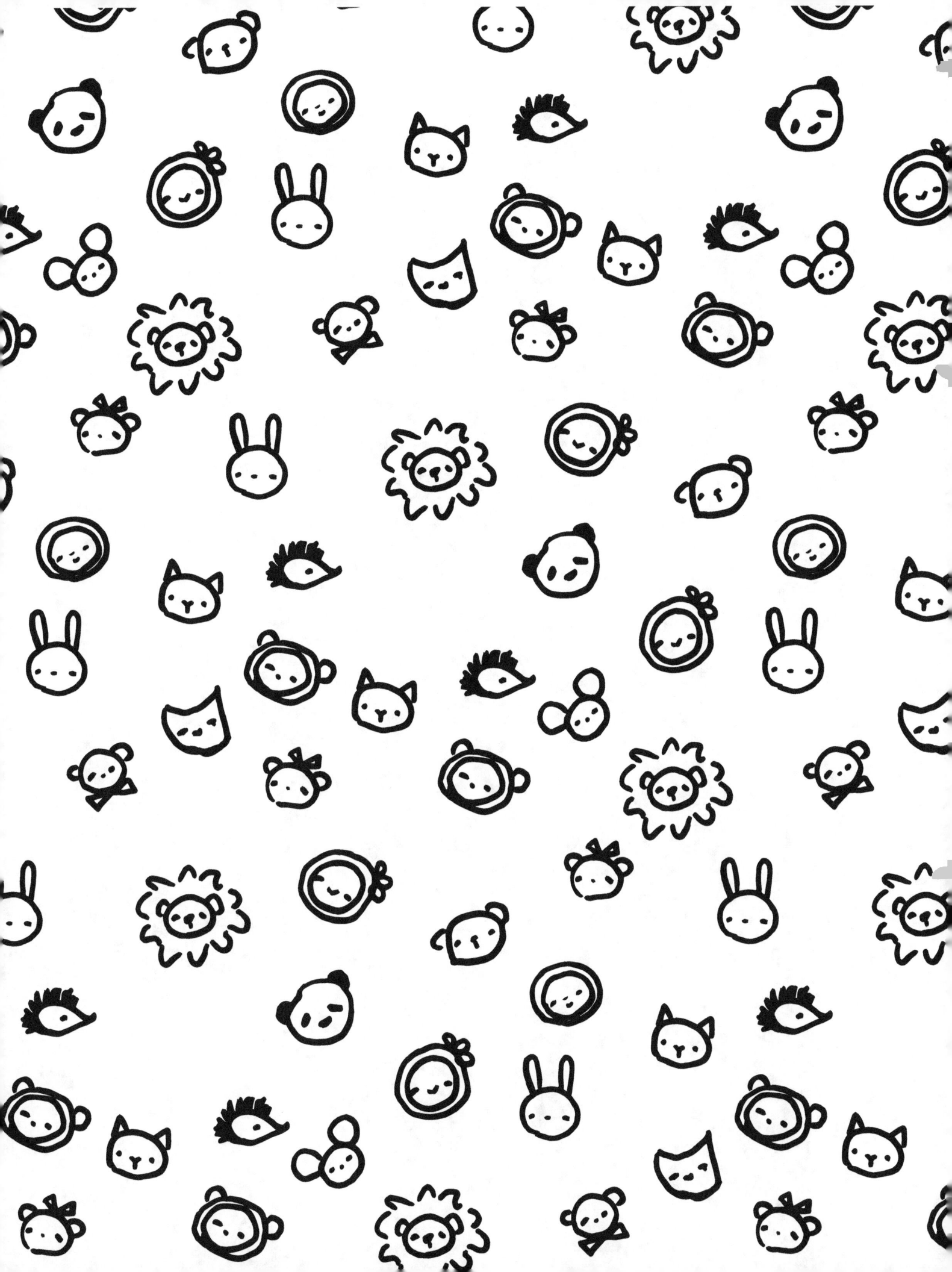

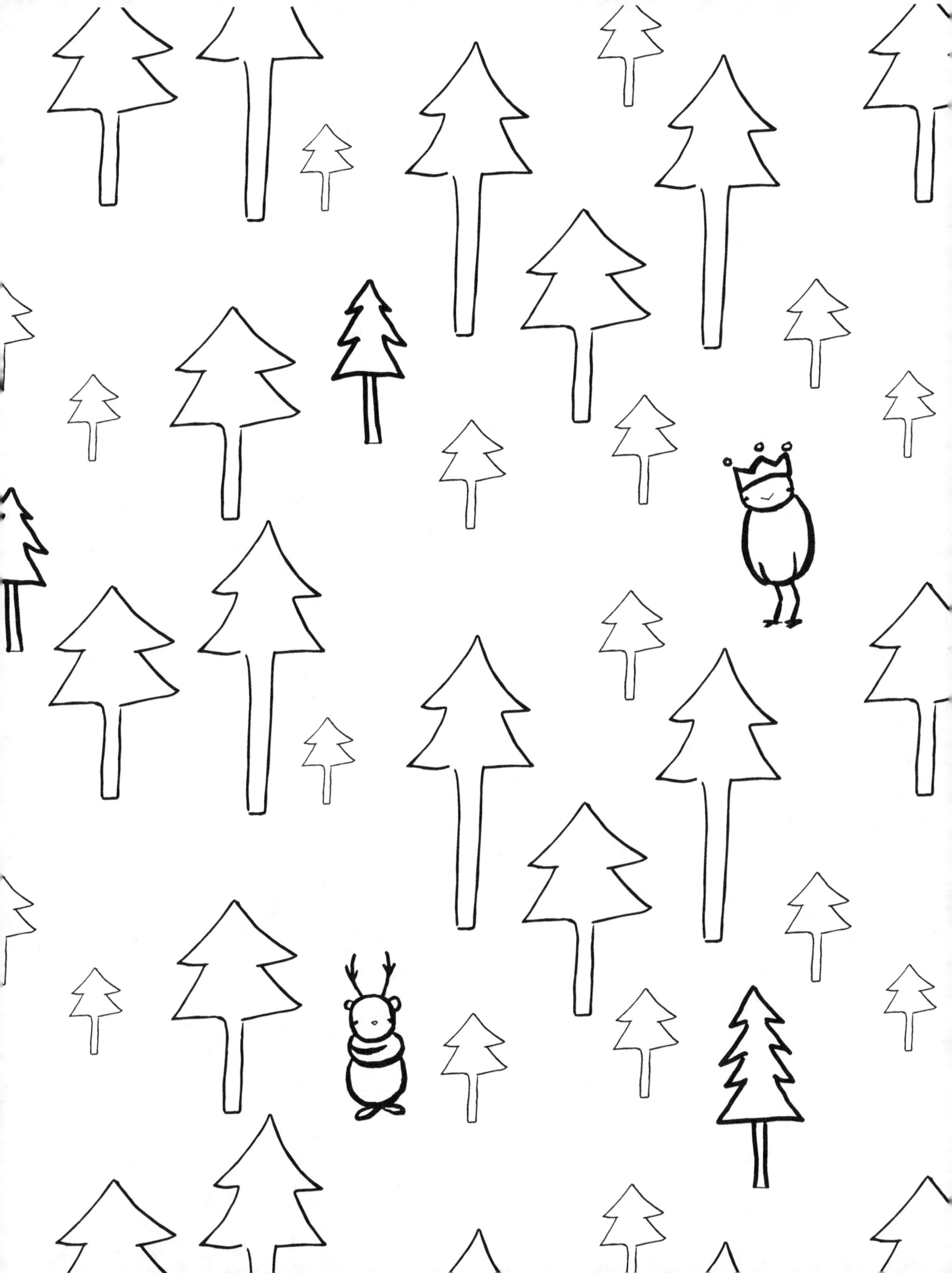

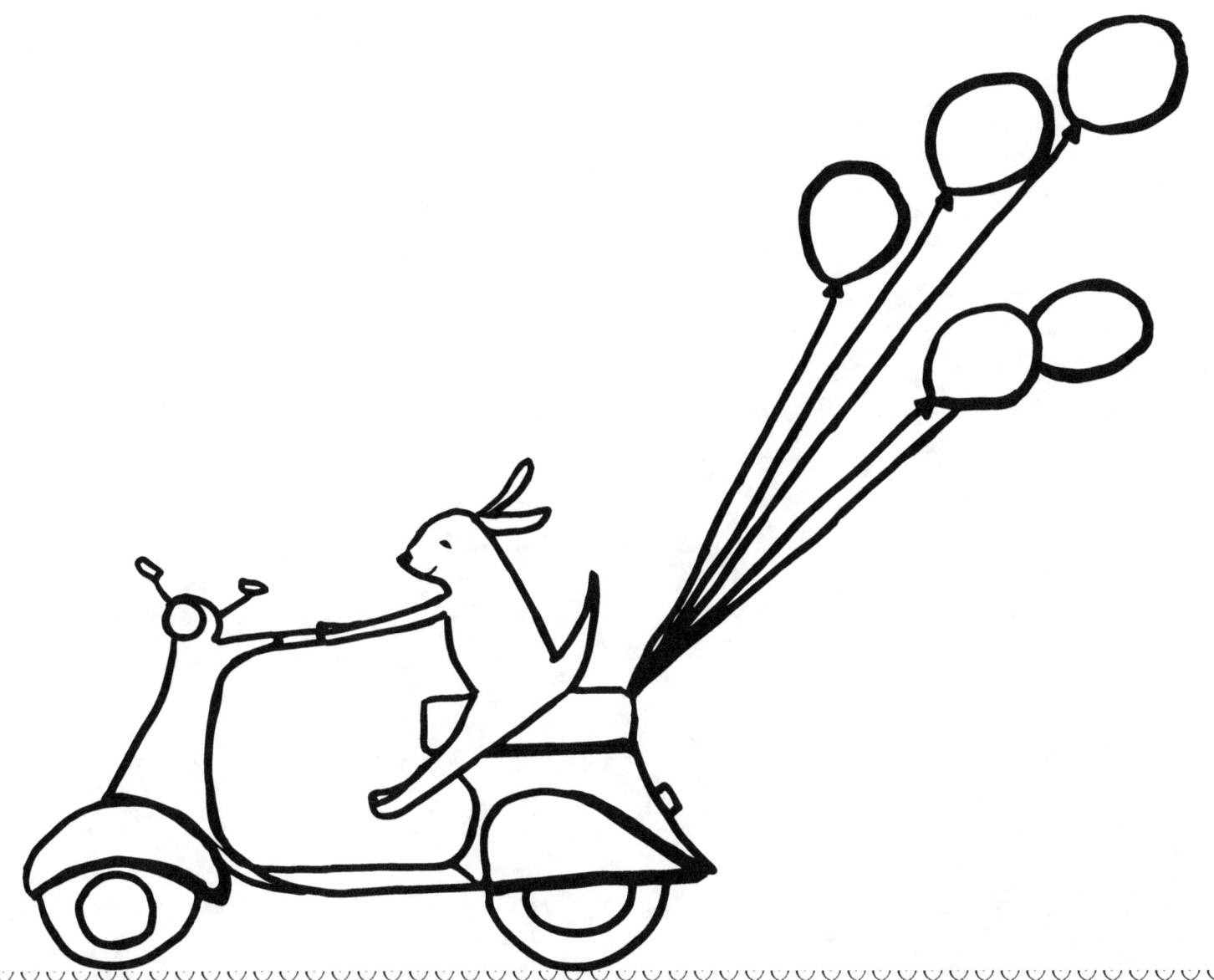

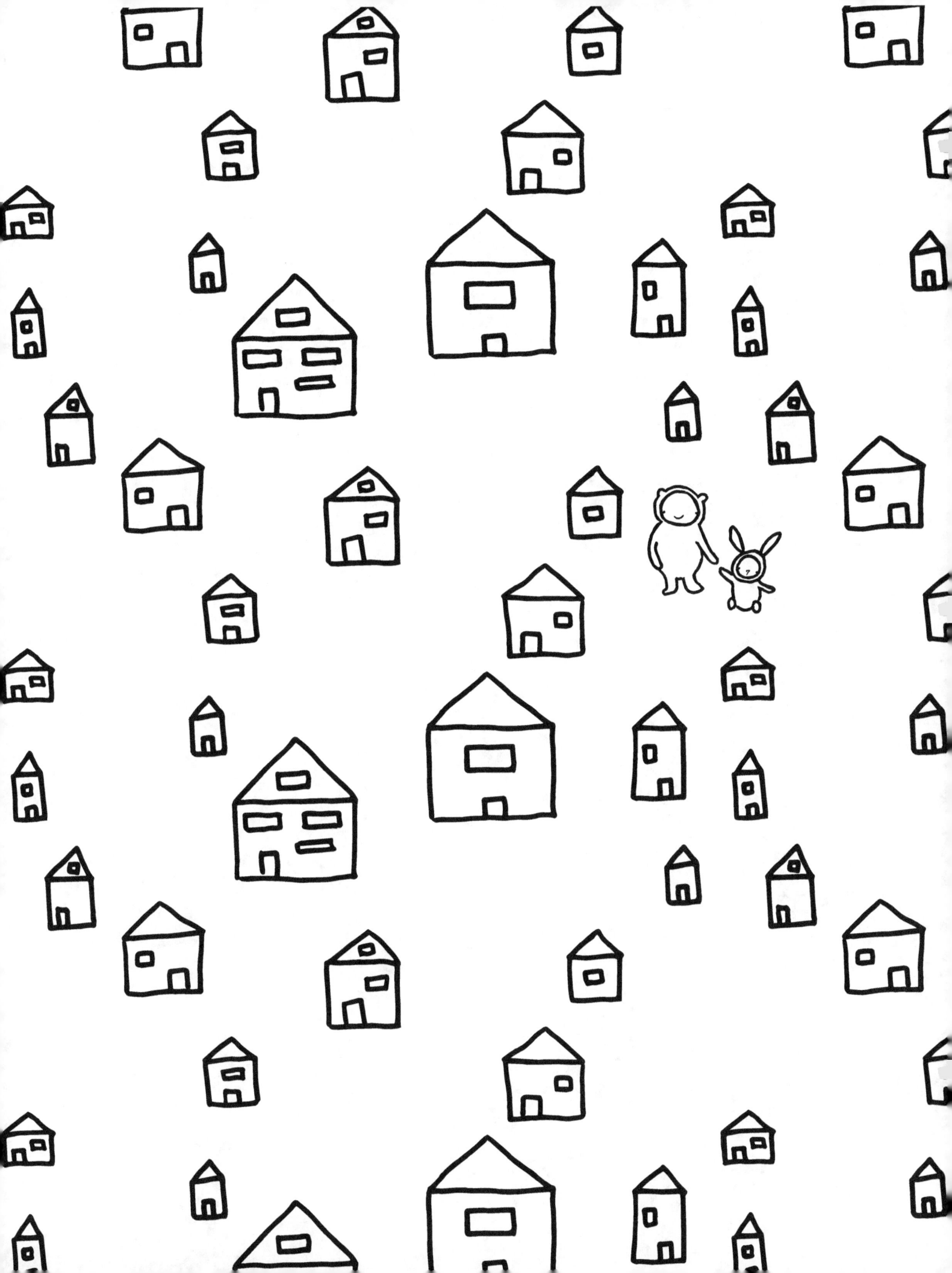

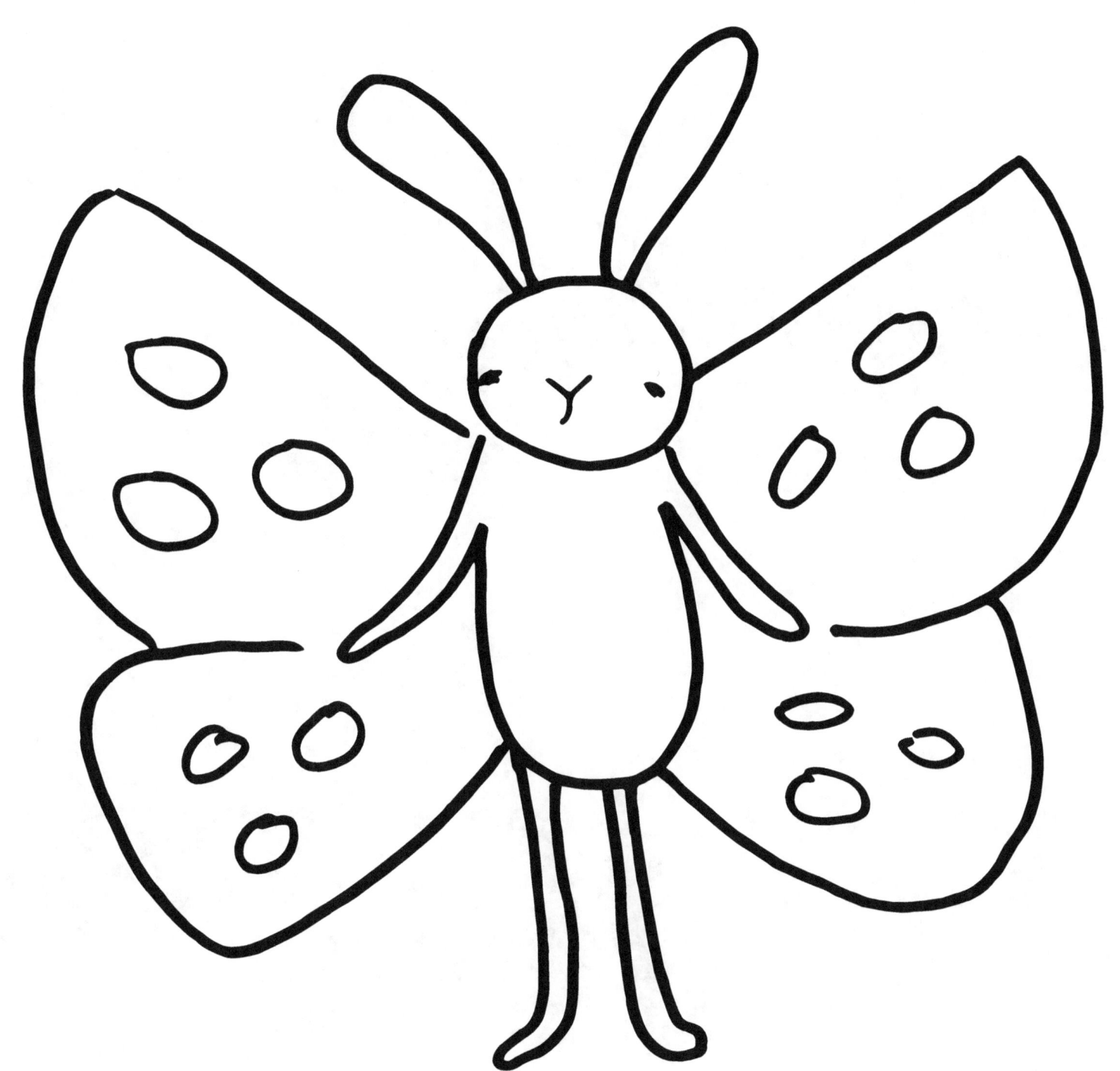

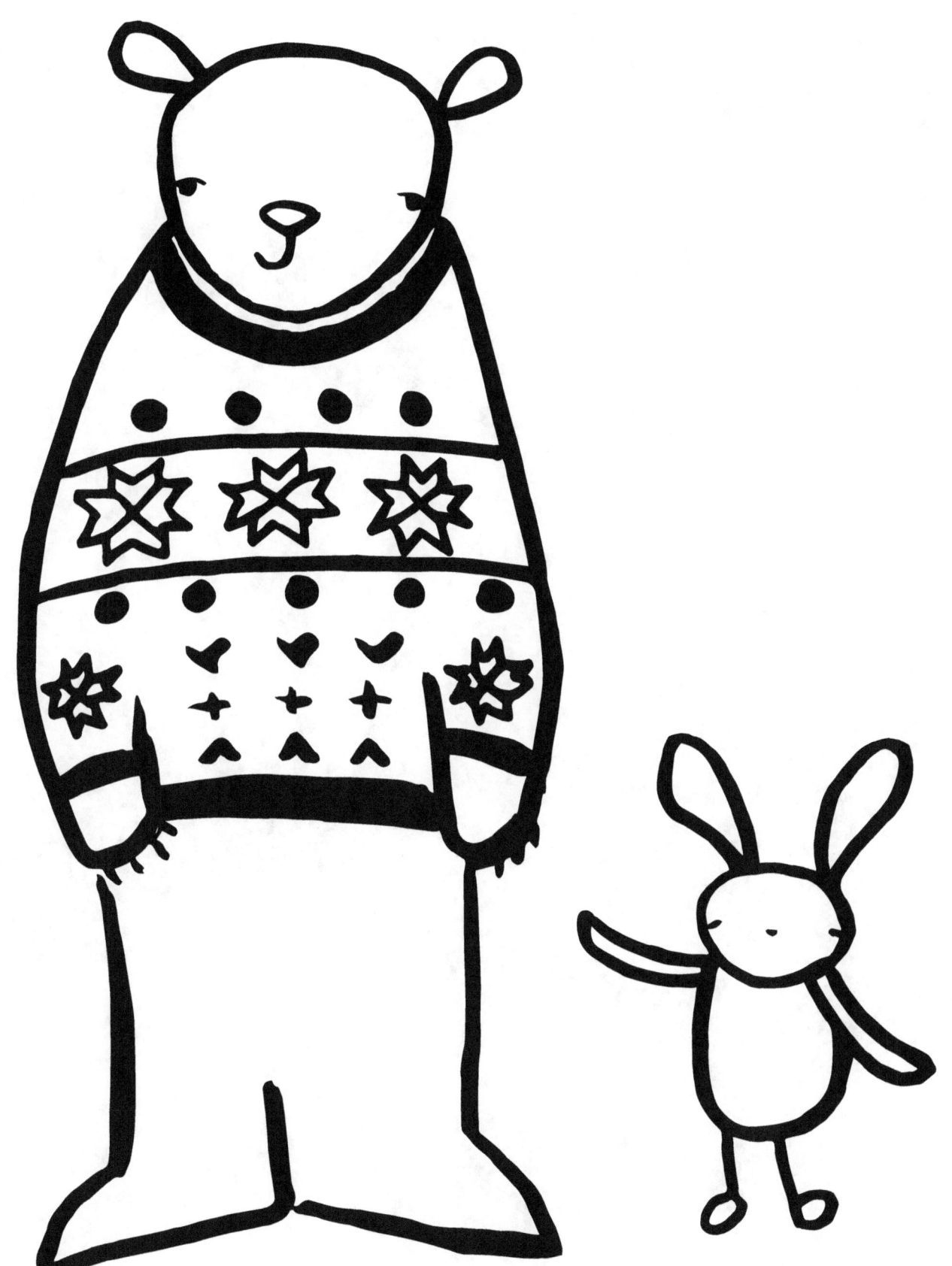

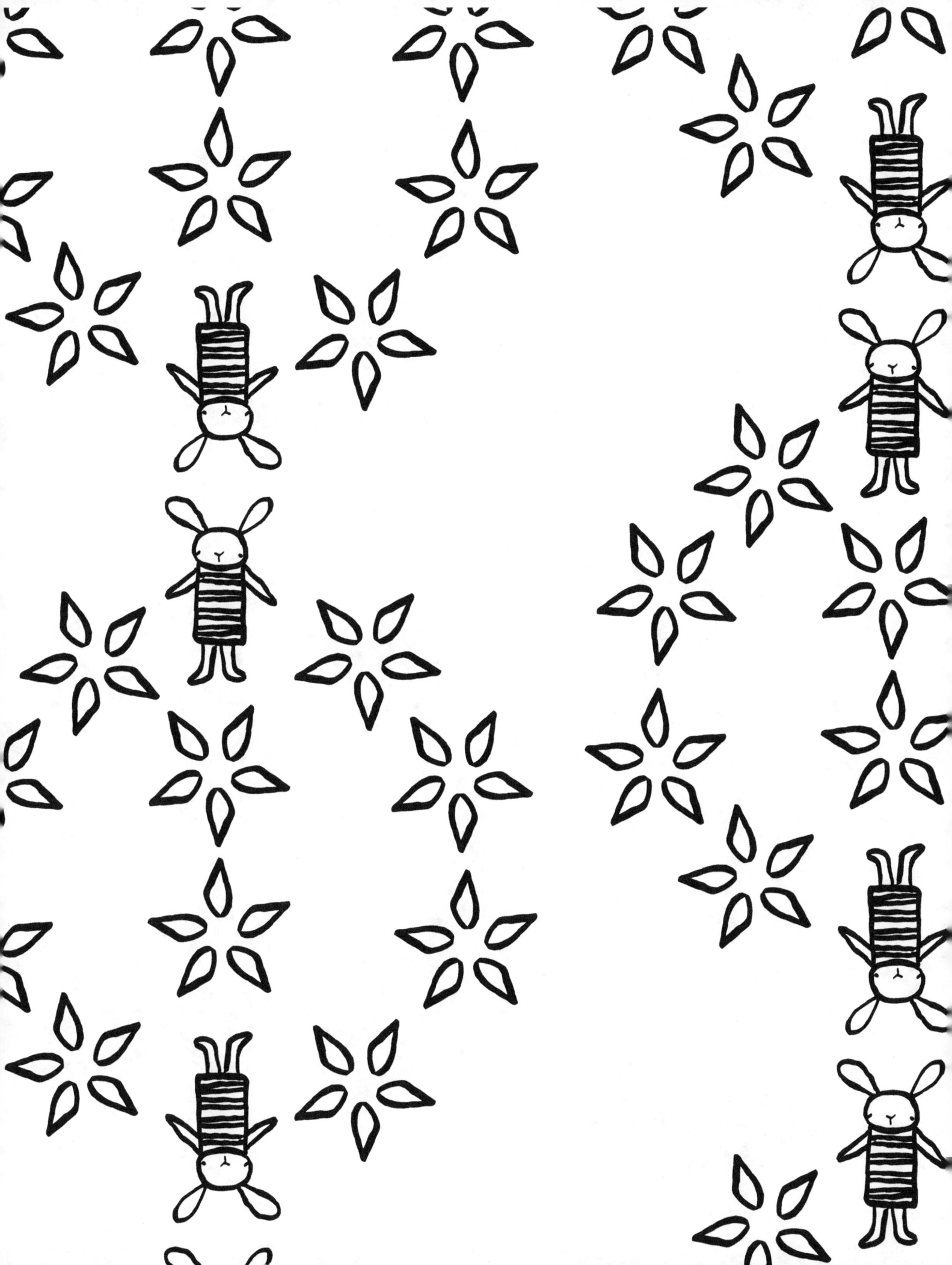

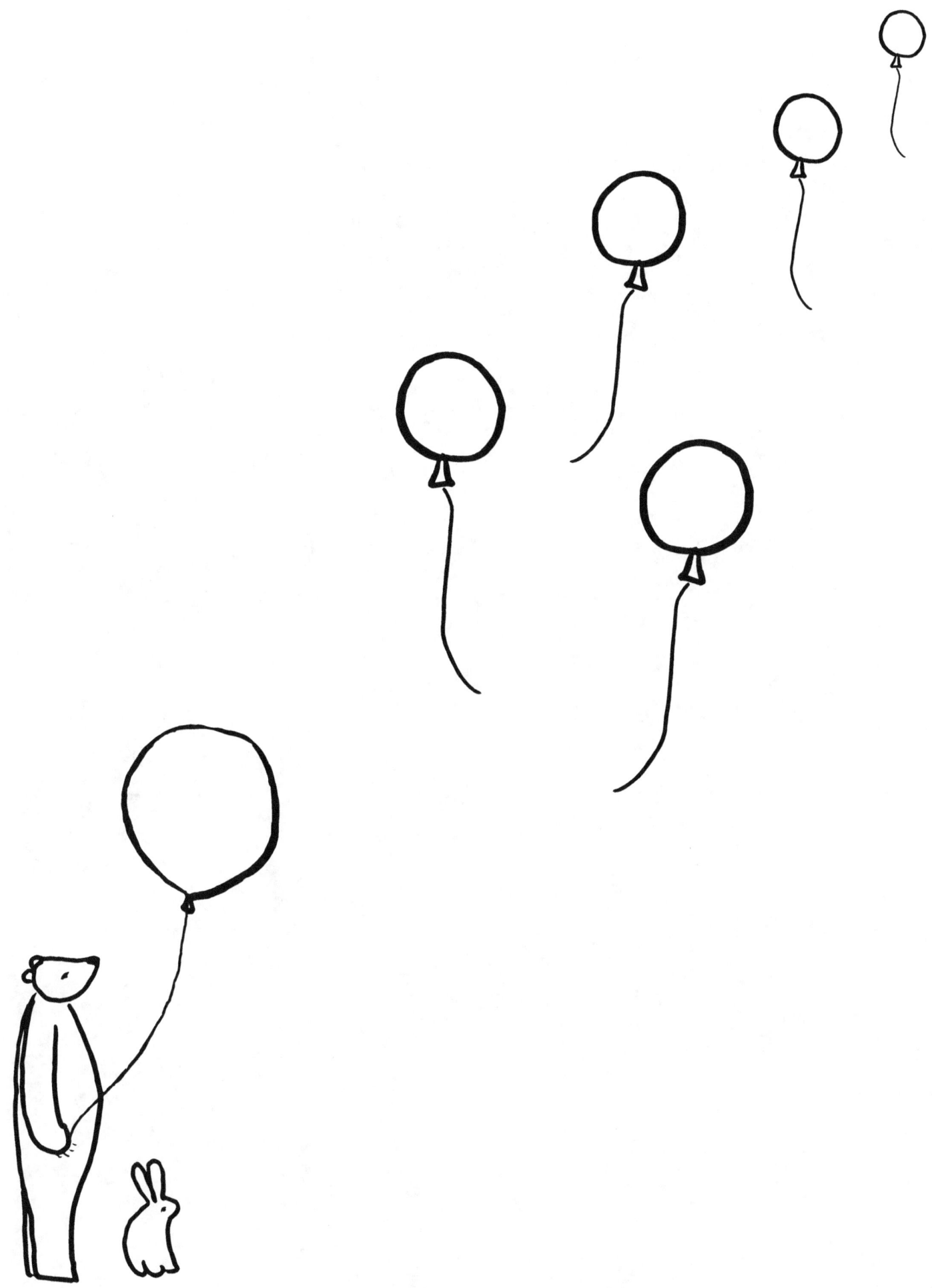

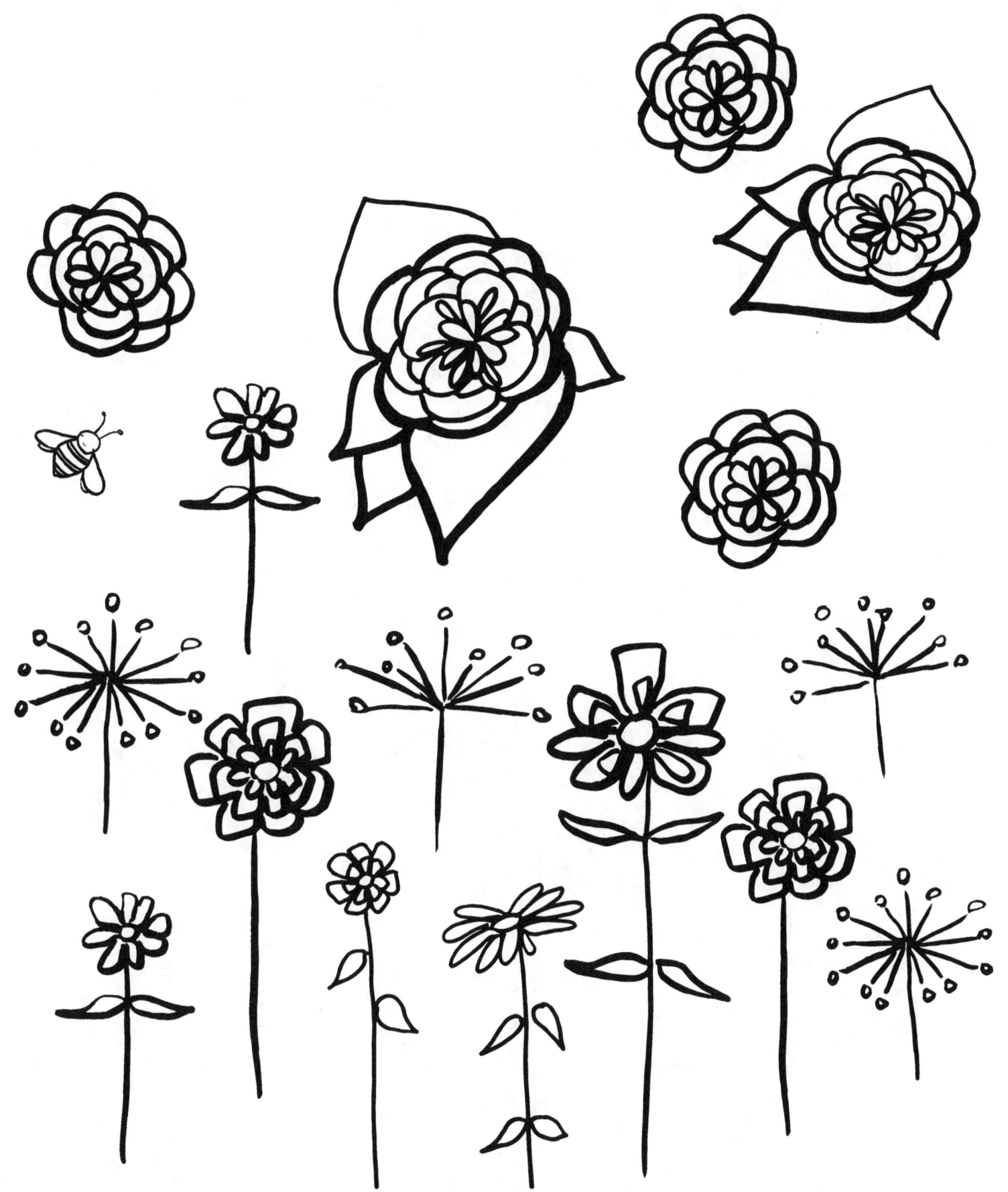

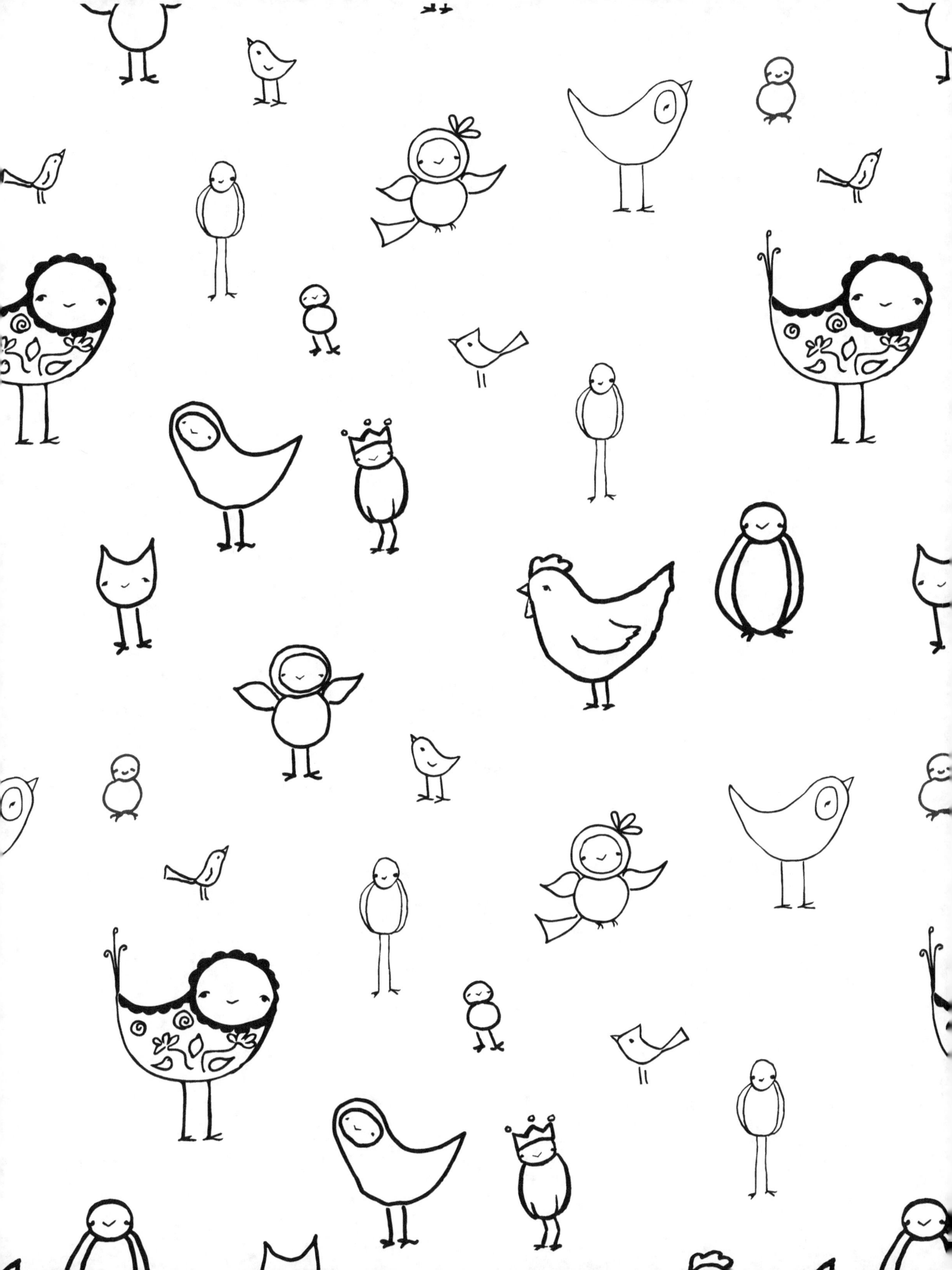

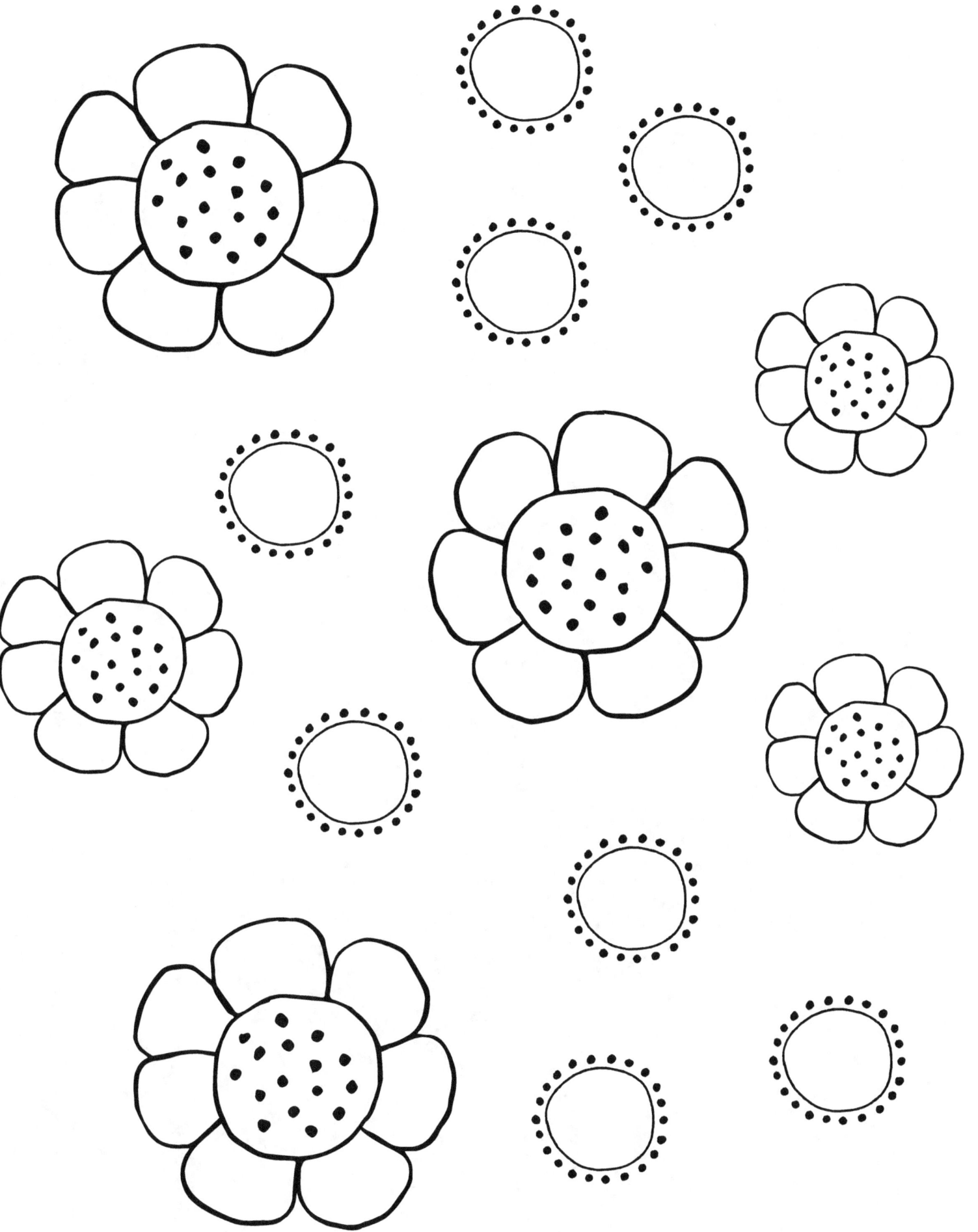

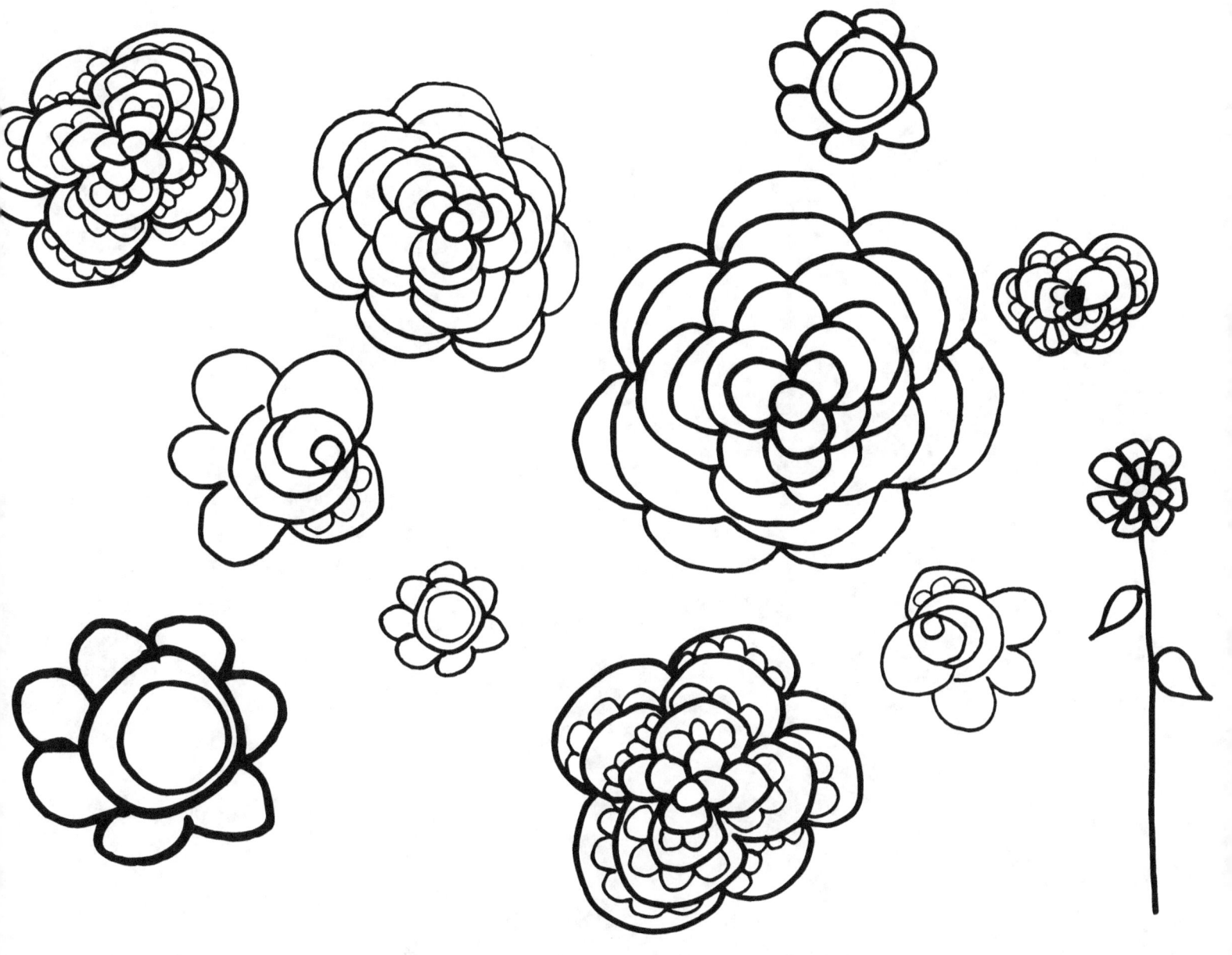

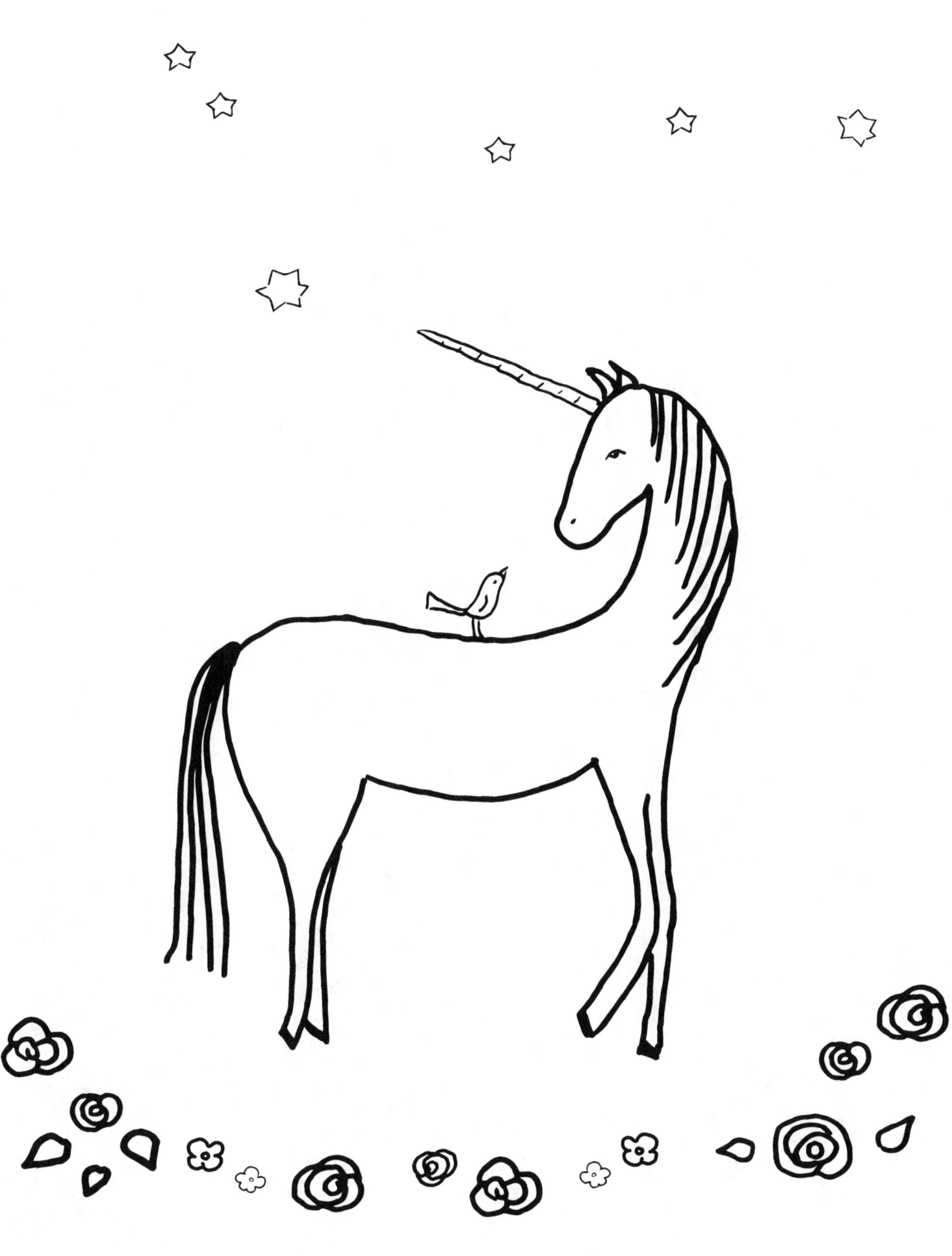

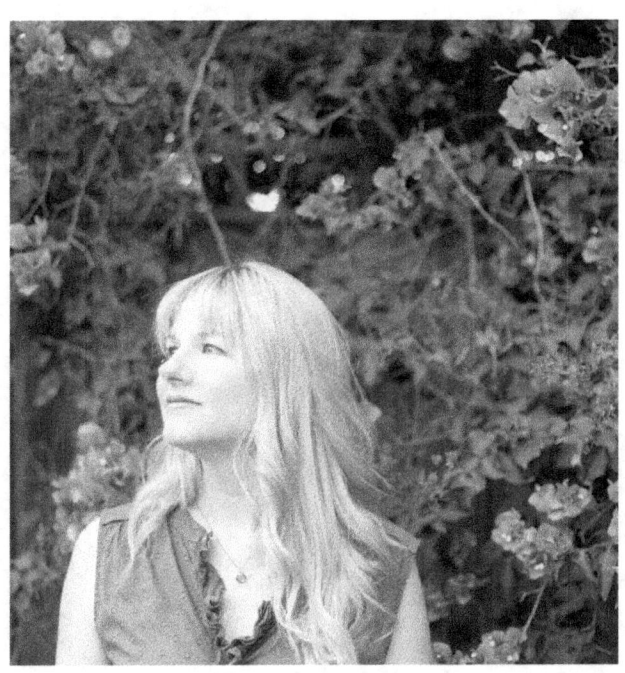

Marisa Anne Cummings is an artist, author, and fabric designer living in Los Angeles, California.
She began Creative Thursday
with an intent to be more creative one day a week.
Now Creative Thursday has become home to
a family of friends who wear hats, hold hands, and encourage you
to follow your dreams too.

Other books by this artist:
Creative Thursday Everyday Inspiration to Grow Your Creative Practice
Marisa's Big Book of Pop Out Boxes

www.ingramcontent.com/pod-product-compliance
Lightning Source LLC
Chambersburg PA
CBHW080932170526
45158CB00008B/2266